"Man is thus his own greatest mystery. He does not understand the vast veiled universe into which he has been cast for the reason that he does not understand himself...least of all does he understand his noblest and most mysterious faculty; the ability to transcend himself and perceive himself in the act of perception."

—Lincoln Barnett

THE LENS OF PERCEPTION

process of working w/the "Lens" (pg. 94)

THE LENS
OF PERCEPTION

HAL ZINA BENNETT, PH.D.

A FIELD GUIDE TO INNER RESOURCES

CELESTIAL ARTS
Berkeley, California

Celestial Arts
P.O. Box 7327
Berkeley, California 94707

This is a "Field Guides to Inner Resources" book, a series
of tools for tapping the wealth of our inner worlds.

Cover design by Ken Scott
Text design by Paul Reed
Typography by HMS Typography, Inc.

Library of Congress Cataloging-in-Publication Data

Bennett, Hal Zina, 1936-
    The lens of perception.

    Bibliography, p.
    Includes index.
    1. Perception. 2. Consciousness. I. Title.
BF311.B448   1987   153.7   87-14697
ISBN 0-89087-492-1

CONTENTS

ACKNOWLEDGEMENTS

Every book is a joint effort involving the author and a number of *silent collaborators*: publisher, author, editor, book designer, typesetter, printer, warehouse staff, general office staff, sales staff, book retailer, distributor—not to mention the author's spouse, friends and readers. When I look at the list of people whose energies I know go into making a book successful, I cannot help but be humbled.

At the top of the list of those I'd like to thank are: my wife Susan Sparrow, whose appreciation and knowledge of the inner world has been an inspiration for me; my editors and friends, David Hinds and Paul Reed, for their faith in my vision and help in refining the finished manuscript; and finally, my publisher Phil Wood, whose special vision continues to support one of the most exciting and fresh publishing ventures in the country today.

The list of people I'd like to thank at Celestial Arts/Ten Speed Press is a long one, and I am afraid that any effort to do justice to that list would inevitably end up with leaving one or two people out. Rather than risk that, I must thank you all as a group, and assure you that I recognize your contribution and truly do appreciate the role you have taken in the publication of this book.

*I dedicate this book to Don Gerrard,
far too modest, whose creative genius gave
a brand new face to publishing,
and whose loving friendship I greatly value.*

FIRST:

The Inner Landscape

> *"A new vision is emerging of the possibilities of man and of his destiny, and its implications are many..."*
> —*Abraham Maslow*

Philosophers since the beginning of time have reflected that true self power comes not through controlling objects or people outside us, and not from blindly following the examples of others who have gone before us, regardless of how successful they may have been, but through identifying and making use of our own inner resources. It is only by tapping our own inner resources, and making use of those human qualities, human strengths, and human weaknesses that make us each who we are, that we truly come into our own to enjoy the rewards of self-power.

In spite of the abstract awareness of these truths, modern civilization has not always known how to apply this knowledge in everyday life. Most of our attention has been given to exploring ways of bettering ourselves through opportunities offered in the external world. And until very recently in our history, the external opportunities—land, natural resources such as coal, gold, oil, new technologies—offered so much, we had neither the time nor the motivation to look inward. At best, we have focused attention on inner resources such as "aptitude" for a specialized career or field of study. We speak of having an *aptitude* for mathematics, or for writing, or for teaching, or sports, or science, or art.

Although it is true that aptitudes, as we speak of them here, are personal resources, they are only small, though important, pieces of the puzzle. Inner resources include our dreams, our aspirations, our fears, even the contradictions in likes and dislikes that so often cause us bewilderment, indecision, and conflict. In short, our inner resources include anything which might emerge from the human consciousness.

The great explorers of the inner world, everyone from Homer to C. G. Jung to contemporary researchers like Roger Sperry and Carl Pribram, have paid homage to the vast and often mysterious functions of human consciousness. And yet, no-one can quite define what consciousness is or give concrete proof that it really exists. It affects every moment of our lives, yet we can't put our fingers on it or dissect it as one might dissect a human heart or a kidney or the human brain. We can experience consciousness through dream, accepting the fact that without consciousness dream could not exist. We can look at the choices we make in friendships or lovers, and see that yours and mine are significantly different—and the differences in those choices are a function of consciousness. The evidence for consciousness, then, is found not in the thing itself but in the events and personal expressions produced by it.

In this book, I explore one aspect of human consciousness, that part which distinguishes you from me, that part that provides you with your unique identity. I call this the "Lens of Perception." It is the part that causes us each to think and act in a unique way, making you *you* and me *me*. It is that inner world of people and places that populates and gives shape to your dreams. It is the part that allows the two of us to share the same event in the external world and yet experience it in two significantly different ways. It is the part that contains the resources that you bring to this world, and which the world has never quite known before. Perhaps most important of all, it is that part of human consciousness that provides *inner guidance* which, like the automatic pilot on a great ship, gives us the course home, the navigational instructions to follow the route by which we can fulfill our individual destiny.

We each have a gift to bring to this world, a gift that is essential to the world at this time. There are many impediments, however, to our being able to identify that gift and then commit ourselves to it. We may be fearful that we may starve if we do, or that others will not like us, or that life will become more difficult. The irony is that all these may well be true if we embrace this path, committing ourselves to fulfilling the vision for which we were intended. Those same things will also be true if you embrace any other path, be it one dictated by our parents, or by society, or by a spouse, or for the sake of our children, or even by a spiritual teacher. We will always have fears. There will always be those who do not like us. There will always be times when life is difficult. And yet, through embracing the Lens of Perception, we discover self-love, love in a form that cannot be surpassed, love that goes out into the world as actions that matter, creative and loving acts that truly light up our own little space in the universe.

At the age of five or six, I recall having my first glimpse of what I now call my Lens of Perception. It occurred rather spontaneously and certainly not at a time when I was looking for it. One day, exploring an empty barn near my home, an older playmate and I found some round, organic-looking sacks, broken open at the top. My friend told me they were "birth sacs." We had stumbled upon a place where some small animal had given birth to its offspring—a rat, a skunk, perhaps a cat. All of the birth sacs were empty but one. That one had a tiny pink animal shape inside, with perfectly shaped paws, a tail, and tiny bumps of flesh where there should be eyes.

For a split second, my perception of the world was jarred. In my child's mind I had put together a belief that new beings—at least human babies—were acquired by going to a place called a "hospital," which I knew very little about. That was my perception, not one I had put a great deal of energy into working out. But upon finding the "birth sacs" in the barn that day, my perception of birth was challenged.

The important thing I discovered, at that moment, was not the truth about birth but the fact that there was a difference between my inner and outer realities. I was, of course, unable to articulate the experience until many years later, but even in my child's mind the implications were fairly clear. There was something within me which simultaneously helped make sense of the world and created a chasm between it and me. My own perceptions were mere illusions. As young as I was, I felt that this glimpse of the truth was extremely important for me to grasp. I wanted to get closer to it, to have it hold still for me, but it was a fleeting thing, not one I could recreate at will.

Throughout the rest of my life, I have pursued that vision, that insight, and it always seemed just beyond my reach. Then, when I was in my mid-twenties, I took a trip to Mexico, where the insight became clear to me, vivid and enduring, giving me an image I could hold in my mind and return to again and again as a kind of guiding principle. In the following pages, I describe the experience of that insight, and show how the vision of the Lens of Perception can be applied in virtually every area of your life.

Though it deals with a very abstract and, some would say, spiritual concept, this is not, strictly speaking, a theoretical book. You will find that it is filled with experiential exercises that translate the more abstract concepts, which are inevitable when speaking of human consciousness, into practical terms applicable in everyday life.

It is my most sincere hope that in sharing the adventure of this book with me you would be tempted to fully embrace the world of inner resources which I have called the Lens of Perception. In that embrace you will find your own gift, and acquire the courage and desire to bring it into reality. This gift, shining from deep within your own Lens of Perception, is your beacon in the wilderness, capable of guiding you and lighting up your special corner of the universe.

In the chapter immediately following this one, I tell the story of the clarifying vision I had in Mexico, pretty much as it occurred.

SECOND:

The Vision

> *"For now we see through a glass, darkly;
> but then face to face: now I know in part;
> but then shall I know even as also I am
> known."*
>
> —I Corinthians

Nearly thirty years ago, I spent a summer in Mexico, much of it in a small village, two hours by bus up the coast from Acapulco. As far as I know, the village had no name but was referred to as "the turnaround," (in Spanish, of course) because it was here that the third class bus turned around and headed back over the mountain to Acapulco. I had gone there on the recommendation of a friend, to escape the modern hotels and the tourist crowd. But I was not entirely prepared for the primitive conditions I met, nor for a certain adventure that came to me. Instead of a modern hotel room, I found myself sleeping on a cot, covered only by a light sheet, just one of seven other rugged souls who had chosen this thatched-roof dormitory over the more elegant accommodations available two hours south.

We always arose at sunrise, helped fold the cots,

then stashed them away in one corner of the room. That done, we sat around and sipped coffee from crude, terra cotta cups as we waited for breakfast to be served by the proprietor and his wife. Eating and sleeping under these conditions created a bond between strangers, despite language barriers. I knew enough Spanish to ask for basic life essentials, and the others, mostly Mexican students from the City, knew enough English to make small talk.

One afternoon, I met a man on the beach who said he was a tourist guide. He offered to take me up to the top of the mountain—I do not think I ever heard the name of it—where he promised to show me the most spectacular view imaginable. The fee for this jaunt was reasonable, as I recall something around ten or twelve dollars, and having nothing better to do, I agreed to go with him.

The man's name was "Sen," pronounced the way the Mexicans pronounce the first part of "senor," nearly but not exactly rhyming with "Ben." Sen was a wiry but strong looking little man, who appeared to be in his early sixties. He wore only faded khaki pants and a red T-shirt with a flying hawk emblazoned across the chest. Underneath the bird, written in Spanish, was the name of a local beer.

Sen was dark skinned, and had long black hair that reached nearly to his shoulders. His face had sharp Indian features, and when he smiled, he revealed two front teeth capped in gold.

Just after noon, Sen packed a small knapsack with staples that he purchased from a *groceria* a short way from our camp. Then we set out on foot in the most casual way imaginable. He pointed to the mountain peak where we were going. It looked to me to be miles and miles away. He assured me, however, that it was a much shorter distance than it looked, and I was not to worry.

We traveled on foot for most of the afternoon, taking what he called "El Sombre"—the shaded trail on the eastern slopes of the mountain, which protected us from the torturous rays of the afternoon sun. The trail was difficult, very steep at times, and not well maintained. I failed to keep track of the time, but we must have traveled for at least four hours before we stopped.

Finally Sen announced that we had arrived at our destination, and he led me to the mouth of a large cave, where we sat down to rest. I would guess that the cave was approximately two thousand feet above the sea. Less than a mile to the west, and seemingly straight down, was the ocean. As Sen had promised, it was a most spectacular view. The steep walls of the mountain amplified the sounds of the waves far below, giving the illusion that the sea might have been only a stone's throw away. From this aerial view— somewhat magnified by a peculiar atmospheric distortion—one could watch the waves rolling gently in upon the beautiful white beach, appearing as they might through binoculars.

It was late evening. The sun was setting, and the sky had turned a deep scarlet. At the horizon, sea and sky blended as one in a symphony of reds and yellows.

Spread out between the ocean and the cave where we sat, I saw a strip of tropical jungle. Here was a world of lush greens, of ferns and palms in varying tones, now wearing an aura of pink created by the fading sun.

Blowing in from the ocean the evening air was cool, heavy with the earthy fragrance of the jungle, of naturally composting vegetation and moist soil, and of flowers which I could not see.

"It is like I told you it would be," Sen said. "Do you agree?"

I nodded, agreeing that indeed it was very beautiful.

Minutes passed; then Sen announced, "Darkness will be coming soon."

It took a moment for these words to sink in. And then the horror of it struck me. We had just spent the entire afternoon hiking up an extremely precipitous trail, along which we encountered many hazards. Several times I had clung to the rock face of the mountain to traverse a section of the trail washed out by storms, risking a fall of several hundred feet. Another time a large snake blocked the trail. Sen chased it off with a stick, all the while assuring me that the snake was not poisonous, though its bite could be harmful.

The realization that I might have to go down this same trail in the darkness startled me. How could I have been so stupid! Why had it not occurred to me, until now, that it would be dark when we returned!

I was furious with Sen. What sort of person would guide me to such a place, heedless of the threat to my well being. Surely he realized it would be dark before we returned. God forbid that he had other ideas, that we were to spend the night in the cave, for example, out here in the wilds.

I then became aware of a deep, groaning roar coming from within the cave behind me, and I leapt to my feet with visions of being attacked at any moment by a wild animal whose peace we had disturbed. I began swearing and jumping around, unable to decide which way to turn. I knew there was a washout less than a hundred yards down the trail, and it was already too dark to cross it safely.

Sen continued to sit at the mouth of the cave, completely unperturbed. In fact, he was wearing a toothy grin that did nothing for my sense of security.

Again I heard the groaning roar from the cave. "What the hell is that?" I cried. "Don't you think we should get out of here?"

"Is it such a bad sound?" Sen asked. "I find it rather pleasant."

"Pleasant!" I said, still searching for an escape. "How can you sit there so calmly? Do you know what it is?"

"It is a sound."

"Of what?"

Sen shrugged. "Who knows?"

At that moment, I sensed that he knew something which I didn't. He'd been here before. Or at least he claimed that he had been. He obviously knew that the sound wasn't a threat to our safety. Or did he? I knew nothing about the man, other than what I saw. He had told me nothing about himself. Where had he come from? For all I knew he could be a complete fool, or a madman—some sort of murderer who lured people out into the wilds where he slaughtered them. After all, who would ever find me out here? Who even knew—or for that matter cared—where I'd gone?

"Sit down," he said sternly, pointing to the empty boulder at the mouth of the cave where moments before I had been sitting.

"Not on your life," I said.

He looked at me incredulously. "No? Then, where are you going to go?"

"I'm leaving," I said. "I'll go back down the trail."

"You're joking!"

"I'm not joking at all," I said. "I've had plenty of trail experience back in California."

"Suit yourself," he said. "But you'll miss the best part of the sunset. Look." He pointed out over the horizon. Against my better judgement I turned to find out what he thought could possibly be so important.

At the edge of the horizon the sky was ablaze with a bright pattern of red and yellow light, twisting slowly into a shape that resembled a spiral galaxy. My breath was literally taken away at the beauty of it, and for a moment I completely forgot my plight.

"My god, what is it?" I asked.

"It is what I promised you," Sen said. "I have kept my word."

In spite of myself I sat down and stared out over the horizon. For an hour or more, I watched as the spiraling colors played at the end of the ocean. It was huge, awesome in its proportions, and seemed to have a life of its own, twisting and turning almost playfully, as though it had an intelligence and was performing a dance with the Earth.

Then suddenly it was gone, and we were plunged into darkness.

The groaning roar rose from the cave behind us, and this time I was able to study it, to listen with a calmer mind. Rather than sounding like an animal, it sounded this time like two gigantic boulders being ground slowly together, emitting a voice from somewhere deep in the earth beneath our feet. I had visions of continental plates scraping against one another, their sound amplified and made more resonant by a long tunnel in the cave.

"Listen," Sen said. "Listen."

I did, and the sound varied, not like a voice so much as like music made by a gigantic instrument whose shape and mechanics I could barely imagine.

"Didn't I tell you?" Sen said excitedly. "Didn't I tell you I would show you a wonderful place?"

He leaned down and picked up his knapsack. Reaching inside he produced a round object which he handed to me. It was too dark to see what it was, but from the size and texture I guessed it was an orange.

"Supper," Sen said, announcing this in a completely matter-of-fact tone.

Was he kidding? Was this really his idea of an adequate supper after our arduous climb to this place? Without comment, I sullenly peeled and sectioned the orange, determining that I would eat it slowly, savoring every bite.

I was aware of Sen rolling his orange between his palms, the peeling still in place. He was doing this in a very studied, very methodical way, and I grew curious. As I watched him, I also became aware that the mountain was growing brighter and brighter, almost as though a huge spotlight was being pointed at us. I looked up and saw the edge of a full moon just emerging from behind the mountain, another five hundred feet above us. This was providing us with enough light to make our way safely down the path, if that is what we chose to do.

I looked at Sen, meaning to suggest this to him. But now he was ripping into the orange like a starving ape, tearing off great chunks and burying his face in them as he sucked and chewed at the fruit. I was disgusted by his behavior, and wondered if he always ate like this. He finished, reached into his knapsack for a bandanna, and wiped off his face and hands, licking his fingers now and then to get rid of the sticky juice. This done, he lay down, arranged the knapsack under his head, and appeared for all the world to be getting ready to take a nap.

"Shouldn't we be getting back while we still have some light from the moon?" I asked.

"What's the hurry? Have you got an appointment with the doctor or something?" To this he chuckled stupidly, like a man unaware of the fact that no one else thought his joke funny.

"When *are* we going back?"

"Why don't you just enjoy yourself," he said. "Take it easy."

I don't know whether I was more angry than anxious, but I could see that there was no sense in trying to budge him. He had his own plans for us, and he was obviously not going to let me in on them. I was completely at his mercy.

I leaned back and started picking at the orange that I had sectioned so carefully. I picked up the first section and was about to put it in my mouth when I felt something moving across my hand. I looked down at the orange section. A tiny lizard, about the length of my little finger, clung to the fruit. I grabbed it by the

17

tail and flung it out into space, disgusted by the thought that had I not felt it moving in time I would have bitten into it, and might at this very moment be spitting out its bleeding carcass.

I was careful after that, brushing off each section of fruit and inspecting it in the moonlight before popping it into my mouth. By the time I had finished eating, Sen was sound asleep. His rasping snores indicated to me that it would be no use trying to awaken him, at least not for an hour or more.

I felt restless and uneasy. From far below us I could hear waves lapping against the beach, and this was soothing. Then, every few minutes the cave made that peculiar groaning sound, a sound to which I had now become accustomed. To pass the time, I decided that I would try to plot how long were the silences between the cave's groans, but after an hour or more I could determine no apparent pattern, and eventually gave it up.

The moonlight slowly faded, and again I became anxious as darkness closed in around me. Now every sound seemed amplified, and I became aware of live things all around me. High pitched whistles from inside the cave suggested the presence of bats. Rustling in the trees suggested night birds, or perhaps nocturnal animals. None of these things particularly disturbed me, though they didn't exactly put me at ease, either. I had spent many nights under the stars back in the states, hiking in the Sierras. But I have to admit that these sounds were not familiar to me, and my inability to identify them put my nerves on edge.

The sky was brilliant with stars, the Milky Way like a great sea of light. Several times I saw meteorites trailing across the sky. In spite of my nervousness, I caught myself dozing, jerking to attention when my body relaxed and I almost lost the balance of my sitting position. At last I gave into it and laid down, staring up at the sky until I fell asleep.

The next thing I knew there was a shriek, and I sat bolt upright, not knowing what to expect. The shriek shattered the stillness once more, and I looked up, having determined that the sound had come from above and to my left. As I searched the darkness, the shriek came again, and a huge bird, with a wingspan of at least six feet, swooped down, coming right for me. I leapt behind Sen's rock—where he continued to sleep soundly—just as the great bird shot by.

As the bird passed, less than a foot from my face, I saw its talons extended as though for a kill. But that was not the worst of it. Just a few feet past me, it stopped in mid-flight, seemed to gather itself into a ball, and suddenly changed directions, facing me once again as though preparing for another attack. I shielded my face with both arms, fully expecting to feel its sharp talons dig into me at any moment. But then it stopped. As it was hanging in the air like a feathery helicopter, I thought I heard it make a sound.

Surely I was dreaming. But I knew I wasn't. I looked directly at the bird and saw that it had a human face.

I rubbed my eyes, certain that what I was seeing couldn't possibly be true. But it was. The bird had a human face. Moreover, it was a face I recognized. It was Sen's face! Sen had taken the form of a giant night hunter. I glanced down on the ground where he had been sleeping. Indeed, he was gone. And there, as clear as the paper on which these words are printed, was the bird—Sen in the form of a bird, hovering before my eyes, flapping his wings gently and evenly as he held his space in the air.

"What are you doing?" I asked, at the moment not thinking how incredible it was to be talking to a bird who had taken the face of my companion.

"Coo! Coo! Coo!" the bird said. This was followed by laughter—laughter that I knew was Sen's. The laughter ended and was followed by his stupid chuckling. Did he somehow expect me to share in his little joke? I didn't think it was funny. In fact, I was shaking like a leaf, still unable to give a rational explanation for what I'd seen. Besides, the bird was still there, still hovering within arm's length of me.

I decided to treat it as an everyday occurrence. After all, maybe it was a dream. I had heard that the best way to stop a person or situation that you didn't like in a dream was to rein in your rational self and tell it to go away. I did this, and heard the bird reply, "Go away to where? You said yourself it wasn't safe to go down the trail in the dark."

"But you're a bird," I said. "You can fly."

"Oh, right. That's right," I heard Sen say. "Goo' bye, then."

And with this, he disappeared. By the light of the stars, I watched him gather his wings under him and plunge off the cliff where I was sitting. I watched as he circled gracefully, changed direction, and disappeared, skimming the treetops in the jungle below me, apparently continuing his night hunt.

Then, startled, I suddenly realized that I was all alone at the mouth of the cave. Could this have actually happened? Had Sen been transformed, somehow, into the body of a bird, a giant owl or whatever it was? In any case, it was very clear to me now that I was left alone on the mountainside.

I heard the crunch of gravel on the path a hundred feet away, off to my right. I called out, "Sen, is that you?"

Much to my relief, my companion came into view, hooking up his pants.

"Where were you?" I asked.

"I went to take a crap," he said. "What's wrong? Are you late for your appointment again?" This was followed by his usual stupid chuckle. Then he went back over to his rock and stretched out, arranging the knapsack under his head, as before.

"I've had enough of this," I said. "Stop fooling around with my head."

"I'm going back to sleep," he said. "Wake me when the movie's over."

I could not believe his audacity or his incredible coolness. Within seconds he was sound asleep again, apparently oblivious to everything going on around him. I lay brooding, angry, thoroughly shaken by everything I had been through that night. I wanted to grab Sen by the shoulders and shake him awake. I wanted to scream at him, to tell him how much I resented the games he was playing with me. I didn't know how he was accomplishing what he was doing, and I didn't care. I just wanted it to stop.

I huddled close to my rock like an animal guarding its territory. I myself began to feel like an animal, destined to live out its life in the wild. I felt a warming sensation throughout my body, a rippling of muscle. Perhaps it was due to a warm breeze emitted from the mouth of the cave. It was certainly possible that there were hot springs somewhere below that occasionally emitted heat which escaped to the outer vestibules.

I found myself staring steadily and angrily at the sleeping Sen. I had never felt such hatred for another man. But as I stared at him I could not identify my anger. I felt a strange fear, like nothing I'd ever felt before. It was as though this man was an intruder in my life, that he was threatening me or something that belonged to me.

I watched him cautiously, waiting for him to make the slightest move in my direction, a move that would indicate that I would have to fight with him, perhaps until one or the other of us was dead. I determined that I would be the victor. After all, I was larger, more powerful than he.

Sen's snoring stopped. He took a deep breath, then suddenly began to tremble all over, as though he was having some sort of fit. The light changed and I saw a giant cat, a mountain lion or a panther standing between me and him, teeth bared.

"Sen," I cried, wanting to warn him. But a strange sound came from my throat, a hissing that I barely could identify with.

Sen sat bolt upright and looked calmly past the cat. In fact, his gaze was piercing, looking right through the cat into my eyes. "Stop this nonsense right now," he said. "You need your sleep. You'll be exhausted in the morning."

"The cat," I said. "Don't you see it?" At that moment I wasn't certain of anything. I could not clearly see the cat myself. It was too close for me to see. I was terribly confused. Why couldn't I see it? I was aware only of its threatening posture, baring its teeth, ready to pounce.

"Of course I see it," Sen said. "It's your cat. It's not going to hurt me."

My cat, I thought to myself. *Mine?* And then I asked, "What makes you so sure?"

"I am just sure. I am just sure." He waved his hand

in front of my face. Suddenly I was calm. I felt spell-bound. "You see?" Sen said.

Sen lay back down, and in seconds he was sound asleep again. I drew back away from him, toward the mouth of the cave. The cat came back into focus for me. It was just me and the cat now. The cat turned, gazed into my face, and appeared to grin.

Was all this truly my own creation? I stared back at the cat. Its face lit up, glowing, as though it had been a plastic mask; now someone had turned on a light behind the cat mask, exposing the illusion. The body of the cat vanished and I was looking just at its face, at that backlit mask. Then the mask of the cat began to dissolve, as though the heat of the light behind it was causing it to melt. Soon it was nothing more than a molten blob turning in space like a star. As I watched, it began to reshape itself into a much more geometric form.

After a few moments its transformation was complete. Round, saucer-shaped, it turned slowly in the space before my eyes. The light still shown within it, as though it possessed its own source of illumination. It turned again and again, revealing its full configuration, thin and elliptical from the side, round and perfectly symmetrical from the front. It was a lens, like the lens from a telescope or a magnifying glass. But this lens had an organic appearance, not unlike a living cell, translucent and soft, definitely alive, a geometric jellyfish.

I moved closer to the lens. Deep inside it I saw movement. What were these shapes? I saw many images from my childhood, my brothers, the house where I'd lived during my high school years in Michigan, my parents, my first lover. I thought about how people often reported seeing their lives flash before their eyes when they were faced with death. Could this be the case? Was I near death? I looked deeper into the lens, as though I might find the answer there. I saw a cat, a powerful mountain lion. There was also a giant bird. There was a groaning cave, and a beautiful sunset over the ocean. There was a rugged trail up a mountain, and a man. I looked more closely. It was Sen. He was sleeping by the rock, his head on his knapsack. I could not figure out where he was—in the lens, or beyond it, or both?

The lens turned in the air. I closed my eyes, trying to block it out, trying to see around it, or to see a clear place through it where the world beyond would not be distorted by the images inside the lens. But I could not escape the lens's influence, and now I was aware that it was turning deep in my consciousness, in the same space out of which dream and imagination are created. I had never before noticed how large this mental space I called imagination could be. It had no limits, no beginning, or middle, or end. It seemed to stretch out in all directions, a vast landscape whose borders were as unlimited as space itself.

At one moment I could be on the mountainside with Sen, in Mexico. A second later I was back in Michigan, many years before, a boy of twelve riding his bicycle on a rainslick asphalt street. A second after that I was driving across the Arizona desert in January, with a car load of friends, all in our early twenties, heading back to California after a Christmas holiday with our families in Michigan. Now I shifted to a backpacking trip in the high Sierras, where I fished for trout on the bank of a mountain lake.

Where was the lens now? I couldn't find it. It seemed to have merged with all the rest, lost in the jumble of everything I held in my consciousness. I felt panicked. Losing the image of the lens was like losing a treasure I had dreamed of discovering all my life. Then there was a long moment of perfect clarity when I realized what had happened to the lens. I saw that it hadn't disappeared at all; the lens *was* my consciousness, not simply a piece of it.

For a long time I just sat quietly and thought about this. It seemed to me that the lens was like a vehicle for my awareness, giving me an identity separate from the rest of the world. This was the image I had been seeking since I was a child. A thousand questions and speculations that I had entertained along the way now focused on this lens image for me.

Having the sense of separateness which the lens provided seemed to me both exciting and frightening. It meant that I was not like an ant, with instincts, that is, pre-programmed responses built in, dictating my every action. It meant that I was capable of creating my own program, or even of overriding whatever biological or God-given programs might be built in.

My decisions, my fears, my dreams, my acquired knowledge—all could come into play. In my present situation, up on the mountain, I could make a decision, based on my fears or on other factors contained in my lens, to leave my guide sleeping by the mouth of the cave and make my way down the mountain trail alone. Or I could choose to trust him and wait for morning. Regardless of which decision I made, my awareness of my separateness—achieved through the lens—was now very clear to me. I alone was responsible for my destiny. I was terribly excited about being able to see all this. The vision of the lens provided me with a symbol for making sense of knowledge I hadn't even been aware that I was collecting over the years. I wanted to awaken Sen and discuss it all with him.

"Sen," I said. "Sen, are you asleep?" I went over to him and gently shook his shoulder.

"What do you want?" he asked, turning his head to face me. "Have you created another cat? A bird?"

I started to look for the words to explain what I was seeing. But then I backed away. I realized that Sen already knew about everything I had seen. To him it was common knowledge, and he had no time for it. "Never mind," I said, deeply hurt by the realization that I had no one with whom to share my discovery. "I'm sorry to disturb you."

Sen mumbled something I couldn't understand and went back to sleep.

I sat down and watched the world beyond the lens, and saw it all merge with memories, images, ideas, and feelings that I knew belonged only to me.

As my companion slept, the shadows shortened on the ledge where I sat, and I saw that the Lens was not something new in my life. I saw it far more clearly than ever before, and *that part* was new and unfamiliar, but the subtle mergings of external sights, sounds, and sensations all seemed normal, automatic, even familiar to me. I realized that these things had always occurred—and the only difference was that now I could see them, could feel their shifts and mergings, their constant metamorphoses from one form to another.

I remembered many times in the past—all through my life—when I had also had brief glimpses into this basic truth about our way of processing reality—glimpses never more substantial than the sun's reflection from a bright chrome strip on a passing car. I now saw why life really was not all that it appeared to be. Rather, it took on meaning only as it merged with our images inside the Lens.

Later that afternoon, as we made our way back down the mountain, Sen listened patiently as I related the story of what had happened to me up on the mountain. I wanted to know if he had experienced any of it. Were the things I had seen a shared reality? Had he seen any of it?

Sen shrugged. He was vague and elusive. He told me that the Indians believed that the place where we spent the night was a *sacred spot*, and that people often had visions there that changed their lives. I asked if he had ever had visions there.

"Oh, yes," he said. "That is why I sleep when I go there. When I sleep it does what it must do and I am not always jumping up and down thinking I have to do something about it." He laughed. "Unlike you, I am a very lazy man."

When I tried to get him to explain this to me, he said it wasn't important. He told me my Spanish wasn't good enough to understand him if he really tried to go into it. And his English wasn't good enough for him even to attempt it in my language.

He dismissed me with that phrase the Mexicans have for stopping all further conversation on a subject: "*No me importa*"—it is not important to me. "You went to the mountain, and you saw what I promised you. I am a very good guide. I hope you will tell your friends about me."

I promised him I would.

When I got back to the camp where I was staying, Sen disappeared down the beach, and I never saw him again. I asked the owner of the *hostel* about him. He told me that Sen was an Indian, and that I was lucky to have come back from the trek at all. Sen belonged to a tribe that still lived in the mountains, and they were not known for their friendliness toward *gringos*. They had no respect at all for the laws of the government, and they lived their lives completely cut off from the rest of the world.

I always took this warning with a grain of salt. After all, if Sen's people were so isolated from the rest of civilization, how had he learned English? He knew my language far better than I knew his. Moreover, when I thought back on it, I could not think of a single incident in which Sen had acted in any way that I considered directly harmful. Any harm that could have come to me would have come from my own Lens, distorting reality in ways that could have caused me to use bad judgement and perhaps bring me to harm through my own actions.

The experience has stayed with me throughout my life and became something far more than an unusual memory. The Lens has become a reference point for me, a kind of metaphor over which I puzzled for many years. Only in recent years has it become comfortable for me to write about it, to relate the story to others so that I might share the revelations that have come from it.

THIRD:

Whence The Imprisoned Splendor May Escape

> *". . . and so reality is not that external scene
> but the life that is lived in it."*
> —Wallace Stevens

Imagine that it is early in the morning, and you are standing next to me on that mountain in Mexico. Take a deep breath, relax, and enjoy this little fantasy. We stand at the mouth of the cave, looking out over the ocean. The sun, rising behind us, casts a long shadow over the thick jungle between us and the beach. It is cool. A light breeze flows gently in from the sea, smelling of sea salt, rich with oxygen provided by the thick vegetation all around us.

The view from our vantage point is spectacular. In the cool morning air the long beach, curving out to sea to the north and south, looks crisp and clear and inviting. In another hour the sun will begin to bake the bright sand, and from this distance shimmering heat waves will turn the beach into an Impressionist's landscape, painted with a soft, wavy brush that obscures the edges of everything. There is a large sailboat heading out to sea from a tiny port down left in our field of vision. The boat has a large white mainsail and a light blue flying jib that billows out in front of the boat like a parachute caught in the wind. You can see only one person aboard, a tiny figure at the helm, piloting the boat out past the breakers toward open water.

You hear the chatter of scolding monkeys from the jungle below, but try as you might, you cannot see any signs of such animals amongst the dense vegetation at the foot of the mountain. Sen, our companion and guide, is sleeping, but now he stirs, opens his eyes and looks up.

"Now there are two of you," he says. He is not displeased. He is only noting a fact, though with a slightly bemused expression on his face.

I ask him how soon we can leave.

"You can leave any time you wish," he says, a slightly irritated tone to his voice. "What goes on here is your business. I am *your* creation, just as this mountain is, and the ocean is, and the chatter of monkeys in the jungle is. Why must you ask my permission?"

He is right, of course. None of what you have created exists except in your consciousness. All this is taking place on your own *Lens of Perception*, a lens like the one I described a few pages back.

The mountain I create through the words on this page, or the mountain where you might stand in Mexico, must be duplicated in your Lens of Perception before you can enter the experience. You move about on the mountain in your mind, gazing out over your mental ocean, and even the eyes and ears and mouth and nose and skin receptors you use to perceive are created in that Lens. Take a step forward on your mental mountain. Turn around and face the cave. With which eyes do you see the dark opening in the side of the mountain? With what ears do you hear the groaning voice that comes from deep inside the cave?

At this point you and I share this vision. You might be inclined to credit me for creating this picture, but without your ability to read my words and translate them into the illusion of sensations in your own consciousness, you would be unable to experience anything I might write, and indeed anything that the physical world has to offer.

Whether the experience is imaginary—as we have created through the words printed on these pages—or an actual landscape, such as you might experience if you traveled to Mexico and stood on the very place where I had stood, the process is the same. It is not my words nor the landscape *out there* but the landscape you create in your consciousness—and the self you create in your Lens to perceive that landscape—that provides you with the experience.

In perceiving anything at all, human consciousness also experiences sensations which are qualities of consciousness alone. These sensations are products of the Lens of Perception, projected on the landscape before us so as to clothe the naked outer world. All of that outer world is thus perceived as having qualities which in reality belong not to it but to the human consciousness. We give nature credit for qualities which, in truth, belong only to us, created by our own Lens of Perception. Reflecting on this same phenomenon, the American mathematician and philosopher Alfred North Whitehead once said:

> The poets are entirely mistaken. They should address their lyrics to themselves, and should turn them into odes of self-congratulation on the excellency of the human mind. Nature is a dull affair, soundless, scentless, colorless; merely the hurrying of material, endlessly, meaninglessly.

And the poet, Robert Browning, touched by the same thought, reiterates:

> *"Truth is within ourselves, it takes no rise*
> *From outward things, whate'er you may believe*
> *...and to know*
> *Rather consists in opening out a way*
> *Whence the imprisoned splendour may escape..."*

MY BRIDGE, YOUR BRIDGE

Because each person's life experience is shaped inside his or her unique Lens of Perception, each one's way of experiencing the world will be slightly different. I was born of different parents than you. The parents whose faces I perceive when I see the words "mother" or "dad" are very different than the faces you see when you read those words. The place I see when I read the word "home" is different for me and for you.

And might I add that these things will be different even if you happened to be my brother or sister.

No two people can possibly create exactly the same Lens, not even if they happen to be identical twins. Having been brought up in a different locale, being constitutionally sensitive to different things—so will each lens contain different imagery. And even if it were possible to duplicate all that perfectly, it would not be possible to duplicate how each one of us puts all the ingredients together. The material in your Lens is plastic; that is, you can put it all together in a variety of ways.

Let me guide you through an experiment that will demonstrate this observation:

At this moment, bring one of your parents into your Lens. It may be your mother or your father. Now recall a very pleasant experience with them, say a moment when the two of you enjoyed a vacation together. Explore your picture or feelings of your parent at that time. What kind of person would you say they were? Hold that experience in your mind's eye until you are completely sure that you will remember it.

Now think about a moment when you and the same parent had a serious disagreement, or when they did something that thoroughly displeased you. Explore your picture or feelings of your parent at that time. What kind of person would you say they were? Hold that experience in your mind's eye until you are completely sure that you will remember it.

Now compare the two images of your parents. Are you not more aware of beauty in the physical features or the personality of the first one than in the second? And note, also, that you are able to create two *separate* parents—though both the same person—placing them side by side for the comparison.

Your parent does not mold your picture of them in your Lens; only you can do that. They give you the raw material of experience, but you are the one who takes that material in and, like an artist, shapes it into experience. And at any moment in your life when you think of that parent, it is the organization of the material inside your Lens that determines your thoughts and feelings toward them.

The infinite maleability of the world inside your Lens all but guarantees that your perceptions will be unique and private, no matter how much you and another person are seemingly alike, no matter how closely you share the same physical environment. Twenty different people can be presented with the same physical reality and report twenty different descriptions of it. In the words of Wallace Stevens, "Twenty men crossing a bridge,/ Into a village,/ Are twenty men crossing twenty bridges,/ Into twenty villages..." My Lens allows me to see things that you won't see, and it blinds me to things that you see clearly.

The Lens of Perception is responsible for all sorts of "distortions of reality." It allows us to perceive things that are not, strictly speaking, really a part of the external world. These may be fears, evoked by a situation occurring in the external world, but belonging only to the observer. They may be hopes prompted by opportunities manifest in actions around us. They may be denials that arise when events in the external world challenge our sense of credulity.

Fears, hopes, and denials may appear on the Lens in any of a variety of forms: the jealous lover, fearing his mate's infidelity, may without realizing it create pictures of that mate in the arms of another man; the entrepreneur, hopeful of great success in her new venture, may create images of her business expanding into a nationwide franchise; and the mother, not ready to accept the news that her child has a serious illness, creates a perception of the doctor as a fool who read the charts incorrectly.

In addition to molding the reality we perceive in our own consciousness, the Lens influences the external world, bringing about change that may be positive or negative. On one hand, it allows the lover to see in the beloved what no one else can. There is no question that there is great value in this, both for the lover and for the beloved. In this case, not only does the lover perceive potentialities in the other, those perceptions can have the effect of actualizing those potentialities, much like turning on a light inside a dark room. The opposite, of course, is also true, that a person's self growth can be inhibited by non-loving relationships, that is, relationships in which intimates, parents, or close friends only perceive faults in each other.

Reflecting on the maleable nature of our perceptions, and the ability of the lover's perceptions to bring out specific qualities in the beloved, Abraham Maslow noted that:

> A husband's conviction that his wife is beautiful, or a wife's firm belief that her husband is courageous, to some extent *creates* the beauty or the courage. This is not so much a perception of something that already exists as a bringing into existence by belief. Shall we perhaps consider this an example of perception of potentiality, since *every* person has the possibility of being beautiful and courageous?

THE ART OF COMMUNICATION

If my reality and yours are different, shaped by two very different Lenses, how can we ever hope to accurately communicate any but the most simple facts to each other! The truth is that communication is very difficult indeed. In some respects we take it far too much for granted, blaming ourselves or the other person when it fails, rather than seeing that the Lens necessitates an effort in both speaking and listening that is much more an art than the simple mechanical process it may at first appear to be.

Consider the distress and disappointment of lovers when after a period of enjoying the illusion that they think alike or have everything in common (their life visions *matching perfectly*), they discover quite to the contrary that they have entirely different interests and priorities in life. That experience is a common one, and a painful turning point in most intimate relationships, from which many couples never quite recover.

The inevitable difference between your Lens and mine, and between your Lens and the Lenses of those closest to you, is the source of much pain. Without the differences of perception determined by the Lens, there would be few conflicts between friends, lovers, business associates, and even governments. (It is not, ultimately, geographic boundaries that cause wars; rather, it is boundaries in our inner worlds, shaped by the Lens of Perception.) And it is perhaps ironic that the healing of wounds created by the differences comes not by resolving the differences and becoming more alike but by looking even more carefully at the differences, acknowledging them as the facts of human existence.

The fact of the matter is that there are very few things upon which two people can wholly agree—except perhaps to respect and love the presence of the other's unique, separate, and independent Lens of Perception. To do that is, in itself, a greatly liberating and healing event in one's life. How does this work in one's everyday life? Here is a simple example from my own experience:

When I sit in my home and look around the room, I am constantly reminded of my wife Susan's presence, even when she is not there. I see a beautiful crystal bowl that she picked up at an antique store a few years ago. She brought it home in a cardboard box, all packed in crumpled newspaper. I can look at the bowl now and appreciate it for its own beauty, but inseparable from its inherent aesthetic value is my memory of Susan's face, radiant with excitement, as she lifted it from its box and held it up for me to see for the first time. The bowl was not something I would have even noticed if I'd seen it in the store. But it was something that Susan would see, would instantly be drawn toward in a shop all cluttered with dusty knick-knacks.

When I walk through the house and allow myself to see the various parts that make up the whole, it is not objects I see, though the objects that are there truly please me; rather, it is Susan's and my presence—made evident by the objects—that intrigues and pleasures me.

The evidence of her Lens of Perception—a Lens quite different from mine—excites and pleases me, filling me with a sense of wonder and love. The objects that she has chosen to decorate our home are deeply personal choices, for the most part, things that move her emotionally. As such, I see them as "proofs" of her Lens of Perception, of how she and I are different, different while sharing common sensitivities. I do not know whether I have come to love her choices because I love her, or if I love her because of her choices.

No doubt both are true.

To duplicate this healing experience in your own life, think of a person very close to you. Now imagine their Lens of Perception. See it first as a duplicate of the Lens itself (without images painted on it) in your own consciousness, perhaps as living, gelatinous material in the shape of a giant disk, just as I described in the first chapter. If that image doesn't work for you, picture it in some other way that you have developed in the process of reading this book. Remember to let the Lens of your friend be blank for the time being.

Think about one object that your friend loves. This might be anything from a piece of clothing, to a car, to a house, or even to a town or other large geographic location. Get as clear a picture as you can of this object. Then place that object in your friend's Lens.

Think about an abstract concept or an idea that your friend loves. This might be a spiritual belief, or a personal goal, or a memory of something pleasant that the two of you shared in the past, or even a piece of music. Place this object in your friend's Lens.

Think about any information your friend may have given you about his or her past. Maybe you have a picture of his or her parents, brothers, or sisters. Maybe you have a picture of a conflict or a pleasant experience that he or she keeps referring back to. Whatever it is, place these in your friend's Lens.

Now imagine that you are standing outside looking at your friend's Lens. In it you can see all the things you have just placed there. Do your best to fill in any other information you might have about your friend. Watch the activity and the number of images in the Lens. Try to see your friend as a child inside the Lens. See them in early adulthood. These pictures do not have to be perfectly accurate; if you don't know exact details, do the best you can to invent them.

43

Stand back from the Lens and observe that it is separate from you. Imagine that you place this Lens in front of a great light, and the images in the Lens are being projected onto a screen in your own consciousness.

You are now looking at just a few of the images that make up your friend's Lens of Perception. Be aware of the fact that they experience life by mingling these images with information coming in from the external world.

Note how different your friend's Lens is from yours.

Say to yourself, "This is my friend's way of seeing the world. This is what he/she brings to my world, which I would not otherwise be able to enjoy. This is his/her unique offering. I shall never ask it to be like mine. I bless and love what I see here, fully acknowledging and accepting its uniqueness."

The next time you are with this friend, recall the image of their Lens which you created. As you spend time with your friend, make an effort to fill in more details. When they make a remark about their likes or dislikes, suspend your judgement of their words. Instead of agreeing or disagreeing, simply add that remark to their Lens. Let some part of your time together be devoted to this activity, letting their words and actions add to the picture you have of their Lens.

THE LENS AS A PERCEPTION OF THE LENS

Although it is a key factor in determining the course of our everyday lives, the existence of the Lens of Perception itself is not easy to prove. Unlike your face, you can't look into the mirror and see it reflected back at you. Nor, when you explore your own mind through introspection or meditation, can you point to any physical evidence for its existence. We are finally convinced that it is there only through our own experience of it, based on the rather nebulous *evidence* that it changes the reality of the thing being observed.

How do we find evidence for phenomena like the Lens, that take up no physical space? How do we establish the Lens as a fact in our lives, if we can't see it or hear it or taste it or smell it or touch it? This is an age-old problem. Just as with elusive concepts such as spirit, soul, God, "life energy," or the physicists' elusive "quark," the usual methods for confirming the existence of the Lens fail us. But perhaps by exploring some of the ways that science and religion approach this problem we can put to rest any lingering doubts about the existence of the Lens. The first exploration involves the field of medical science.

In recent years, modern medicine has been searching for explanations for some of the healing techniques employed in Oriental medicine. For example, acupuncture depends on an understanding of something the Chinese call "chi," roughly translated as "life energy." This energy does not correspond to anything thus far observed in western science. Although they cannot prove the existence of this energy by western scientific methods, the fact that real changes are experienced when the therapy is applied does seem to prove its existence. In his book *Inner Bridges: A Guide to Energy Movement and Body Structure*, Fritz Frederick Smith, himself a medical doctor trained in acupuncture, says the following:

> One way to directly experience energy is to receive acupuncture treatment. The feelings of energy activated by acupuncture are known as *di chi*, which includes feelings of a deep ache at the acupuncture site, or a tingling which courses through the body. It is doubly illuminating to look at a classical acupuncture chart, and realize that the exact locations of the tingling you feel can be predicted in energy meridians plotted nearly 2500 years ago. The tingling is not random but follows well-defined paths.

In the physical sciences there is increasing evidence that the universe is not made up of material, as we once believed it was. Instead, it appears to be made up of "energy" or "potentialities" that cannot be perceived with the senses. Often, the only evidence the scientists can offer for the behavior of the particles or energy being observed is the fact that a larger action, one that *is* observable, does occur and would not be possible without the presence of that phenomenon which cannot be more directly observed.

We have all made use of this kind of evidence in our lives. Think of a time in your past when you stood on the seashore and saw trees in the distance, their branches permanently bent by the energy of the wind coming in from the sea. On the day you observed the trees, there may not have been any wind, yet the branches of the trees, swept back by the winds, provided you with physical evidence that there is, or at least was, a powerful force in the environment that molded them that way.

Sometimes the only real evidence we can offer for proof of a thing's existence is our own *belief* in it, based on our inner experience of that thing. When we cannot offer another person solid physical evidence for our beliefs, we may resort to the use of metaphors, comparing the unknown thing to a thing they already know or accept as true: for example, "electrons are *like* packets of magnetic energy spinning in space;" or, "Spirit is *like* an infinite consciousness that permeates everything in the Universe;" or, "The mechanism that allows us to experience the world around us is *like* a lens upon which are painted all our life experiences, these images always imposing themselves on the reality of the external world." Ultimately, however, it is not the metaphor but only the other person's own experience and belief in that experience which convinces them it is true.

In all these methods, the closest we can come to the truth is by creating a model of that thing within our consciousness. The model exists only in the Lens of Perception. As a creation of the Lens, it may or may not match the external reality it is meant to represent.

When we realize that we must also do the same with our model of the Lens itself, one's sense of credulity is indeed stretched to the limit. To believe in the Lens requires something akin to spiritual insight.

In religious practice, proof for the presence of spirit, soul, or God is described as an "act of Faith." And it is ultimately on faith that we must accept or reject the model I am calling the Lens of Perception. There are those who will have no tolerance for this, resisting the effort to move out of the scientific into the spiritual realm. On this point, I offer no argument. Albert Einstein once said:

> To know that what is impenetrable to us really exists, manifesting itself as the highest wisdom and the most radiant beauty, which our dull facilities can comprehend only in the most primitive forms—this knowledge, this feeling, is at the center of true religiousness.

You need not depend on outside authorities to confirm the existence of your Lens of Perception. You can create your own evidence for it any time you wish. For example, at this moment you could stop reading and imagine yourself with a close friend. The two of you are involved in whatever activity you enjoy sharing.

As you create this experience on your Lens, remind yourself that there is no physical reality of that experience at this moment. The Lens is doing all the work. Although there is no immediate reality to support it, there is an activity taking place on a very subtle level, somewhere inside your consciousness. Your consciousness is painting the picture on your Lens, be it an actual picture, or just the vague and elusive "sense" of the interactions between you and your friend. This is your evidence that the Lens is there, though it is not evidence that you can touch with your fingers, or see with your eyes, or taste with your tongue, or smell with your nose.

CONTRADICTIONS THAT BOND US AS ONE

Some of life's greatest contradictions are created by the Lens. The first one that now comes to mind is the fact that having a Lens that is not quite like any other person's Lens separates me from my fellow humans, accounting for at least a part of the sense of loneliness or isolation we both feel. At the same time, all humans have this in common—that each of our Lenses determine that we will experience the world in our own ways. Second, the fact that your Lens and mine are different means that you may be able to see potentialities in me that I might not be able to see, and through your seeing them, I might be aided in bringing them to fruition. I may also see potentialities in you that you cannot see, and so help you bring them to fruition. Third, communication is made very difficult by the separate realities created by the Lens; however, that difficulty, once fully appreciated, motivates me to look more carefully at the Lenses of those people closest to me. It forces me to see that empathy and understanding—and the courage to get to know another person—are essential ingredients for good communication. Words alone are not enough.

Down through the ages, there have been a number of systems created for resolving some of the problems produced by the Lens. In the following chapter, we'll be exploring four key systems: (1) the viewpoint that the external world is exactly as it is perceived; (2) modern science's efforts to objectify the observer's experience of the thing observed; (3) Oriental philosophy's efforts to "clear" the Lens; and (4) the Shamanic traditions' efforts to embrace the Lens. Each method has flaws. But each one also has elements that are useful for dealing with our separate perceptions in everyday life. Working in concert, the four greatly expand our human potentialities.

FOURTH:

Through The Looking Glass

> *"Now, Kitty, let's consider who it was that dreamed it all. You see, Kitty, it must have been either me or the Red King. He was part of my dream, of course—but then I was part of his dream. . . . Oh, Kitty, do help to settle it!"*
>
> —*Lewis Carroll*

For centuries, great minds have struggled with the Lens of Perception. Truth seekers have been frustrated by it. It is always there, standing between themselves and the external world, distorting what is *really there*. Over the centuries there have been thousands of efforts to invent mental disciplines or technologies to escape the Lens's influence. The following are four major ways this has been done, and they are important to understand because in everyday life we use bits and pieces of them all:

FIRST: There is innocence, that state of mind we enjoy before we are able to see that the Lens is even there, or to wonder at how it affects our lives. In this state of innocence, it does not occur to us that the world might be different than we perceive it to be. This is the Quixotic life, one of "tilting at windmills" with the legendary Don Quixote, fighting battles with enemies that don't exist, and falling in love with phantom lovers, which experiences always, sadly, disappoint. It is also a way of looking at the world which guarantees that we will always feel that everything is out of control, since the world *out there* will always impose a different reality than the one we perceive.

SECOND: There is the scientific method by which we attempt to see around the Lens by inventing "objectivizing" disciplines such as double-blind studies, deductive reasoning, mathematics, the microscope, and statistics, to name a few. However, the further science takes us, especially in the studies of field theory and quantum physics, the more we see the impossibility of achieving this ideal of objectivity.

There are a number of fallacies inherent in science's efforts to objectivize by circumventing the Lens: (1) in order to observe at all you must be "looking for" something. To do this, you create *mental models* within the Lens, and attempt to match up the external world with those models. As useful as this process might be in practical science such as medicine and chemistry, it does warp the truth; (2) on a molecular level the mere physical presence of the observer alters the nature of the thing being observed. Although it could be argued that this would matter only if we were studying atoms, science's own discoveries seem to indicate otherwise. Molecular interactions between the observer and the subject can and do alter the subject's behavior; (3) mental activity is also a molecular activity, and thus when one's consciousness becomes engaged in even the most *objective* observation, there is an interaction between subject and object.

In *Windows On The Mind*, Erich Harth describes the electrons buzzing around in our consciousness, interacting with the external world, as a key issue in science today:

> The observer in the quantum-mechanical world is no longer able to peer unobtrusively through a plate of glass. He must reach out; he manipulates and participates in the goings-on he describes. In doing so he brings about unavoidable and generally unpredictable changes. It is this peculiar interaction between the consciousness of the observer, on the one hand, and physical reality, on the other, that dominates the state in quantum mechanics.

With the advent of modern physics, we entered an era prophesied by William James fifty years ago:

> The divorce between scientific facts and religious facts may not necessarily be eternal as it at first seems. The rigorously impersonal view of science might one day appear as having been a useful eccentricity rather than the definitely triumphant position which the sectarian scientist at present so confidently announces it to be.

THIRD: In the Oriental traditions, there is an effort to clear the Lens, momentarily to erase or suspend the activity that takes place within it. Although it is not usually advocated that this mental and spiritual discipline be used to unlock Nature's mysteries—D.T. Suzuki says, "Let the mysteries remain as they are"—it is interesting to note that in bringing this tradition to the western world, many have adopted the *clear Lens* concept as an ideal of objectivity. But here there is an irony, in that by clearing the Lens, and achieving objectivity, we also erase the ability to know. In the words of Alain, "A mind that could know the object-world without error would know nothing at all."

In the Oriental tradition, one is trained to become acutely aware of there being a difference between external and internal realities, or between the "I" and the outer world. The process of distinguishing between the "I" and the external world might be compared to holding a photographic slide of a landscape up to your eye as you looked through the slide at the actual landscape. The slide would represent your Lens of Perception, the actual landscape the physical reality. In the martial arts you would learn to recognize the picture on the slide as your "inner picture," the illusion created by the "I." And you would learn not to be confused or fooled by that picture. The reason for this becomes apparent if you put yourself in the position of a fencer disciplined in the ways of the East.

Our fears, we know, alter the pictures on the Lens of Perception. For example, you might create a picture on your Lens of your fencing opponent taking a swipe at your head with his sword. You respond to that image on your Lens by lifting your sword to defend your head. But as it turns out, the picture you created on the Lens was wrong. Instead of going for your head, your assailant goes for your midriff. You raise your sword and in the process leave yourself wide open for your assailant's intended attack.

The disciplined warrior learns to respond to movement from the outside world, rather than responding to the movement he creates on his own Lens of Perception. The mind, one is taught in fencing, constitutes a potential "interference," that leaves room for his assailant to strike the deadly blow. The trick, then, is to ignore the "inner voice" or the pictures on the Lens. You treat them as interference, and just as you'd do with a heckler on the sidelines, you respond neither to the content nor the noise or gestures they are making. You literally learn to erase them from your mind.

In Zen, the enlightened state, the state of being which you enjoy after you have learned to ignore the illusions created by the Lens, is called *satori*. Suzuki describes this as a liberation from the "individual shell in which my personality is so solidly encased." He says:

> My individuality, which I found rigidly held together and definitely kept separate from other individual existences, becomes loosened somehow from its tightening grip and melts away into something indescribable, something which is of quite a different order from what I am accustomed to.

In Zen, the Lens of Perception is seen as an encumbrance, and ridding oneself of it, he or she is then able to serve the Higher Order, an exalted position to say the least.

FOURTH: The fourth way of approaching the Lens comes from the shamanic traditions, and it is in this tradition that I will be focusing most of our attention in this book.

THE FOURTH VISION

In the shamanic traditions, the approach is nearly the direct opposite of most other ways of dealing with the Lens of Perception. Rather than attempting to escape from the Lens, with all its "false" influences and distortions, one fully embraces it. However, the ultimate goal of this tradition, paradoxically, is not to hold tacitly onto the perceptions dictated by the Lens, but to get to know them very well so that we are able to be, at the very least, less invested in them. Once that reduced investment is established, we have a choice about acting or not acting on any of the emotional tugs we feel, and we are hopefully better able to see the personal assets and resources available within the Lens.

For shamans, that which occurs within the Lens is perceived as illusion, just as it is in the Eastern traditions. But there is a subtle difference. The student of Zen is taught that the specific content of the Lens, the images that make my "I" different than yours, are not important. The personality is important only in its capacity to distract and interfere. By contrast, in the shamanic traditions, the Lens is a *positive resource*. For example, you may receive through your Lens "visions" that broaden your understanding of yourself or the world in which you live. These insights can direct you in your "right path," that is, the path through which you will fulfill your personal destiny.

In his own understanding of the Lens, the student of the shamanic explores the vision, with the belief that its presence is not without purpose. The essential "meaning" of life is discovered through the individual's exploration of the Lens's contents.

For the shaman, the "I"—made possible by the Lens—serves the universe in the same way that a particular group of cells serves the human body; without that group of cells, the composition that makes up the whole would be altered. Although in the shamanic traditions this abstract concept is generally accepted, it is not one that we can ever fully substantiate. We can't substantiate it because it is not within our capacity to understand how the universe utilizes the "I." Henri Bergson, the French philosopher, stated this concept in terms that are relatively easy for the western mind to comprehend when he spoke of the impossibility of man making a judgement about order and disorder: "That which we may perceive as disorder may be one small element of a much larger Order, which we, in our littleness, cannot hope to understand."

THE WHEELS OF REVELATION

Most Native American cultures utilized some version of a ritual known as the Medicine Wheel. Because this ritual provides us with a clear illustration of the shamanic view of the "I" and its relationship to the Lens of Perception, I present it here in some detail:

The Medicine Wheel took many forms, the most formal one being a congregation of people sitting in a circle. Hyemeyohsts Storm's descriptions of the Medicine Wheel parallel definitions of what modern psychologists call "projective devices"—events or situations that reveal a person to himself. Storm says:

> Any idea, person or object can be a Medicine Wheel, a Mirror, for man. The tiniest flower can be such a Mirror, as can a wolf, a story, a touch, a religion or a mountain top. For example, one person alone on a mountain top at night might feel fear. Another might feel calm and peaceful. Still another might feel lonely, and a fourth person might feel nothing at all. In each case the mountain top would be the same, but it would be perceived differently as it reflected the feelings of the different people who experienced it.

To get a taste of how the Medicine Wheel works, imagine that you have been invited to a meeting of your peers. In your Lens, create a picture of this meeting taking place in a large room, or in an outdoors environment, where you feel safe, comfortable, fully at ease.

All the members of the group form a circle, each one close enough to people at their right and left so that they could easily reach out and touch them. You look around the circle. There are many familiar faces here. There are also some unfamiliar ones. Some faces are friendly. Next to you is a close friend. Across the way is a person you went to school with. There you see a person who cheated you out of some money. Over there is a person whose name was in the paper last year because he was on trial for manslaughter. The circle includes all kinds—ranging from sinners to saints.

A man steps to the center of the Medicine Wheel. He looks familiar to you, and as you study him more closely you see that it is Sen, with whom you have become familiar in this book. He holds up his hand to get everyone's attention, and then he gives the following introduction:

"As we take our places in this circle we voluntarily let go of the perceptions that serve us in our everyday lives. There are people here that we would trust and embrace as our equals, worthy of our love. There are also people here that we cannot trust because they have the capacity or desire to harm us, and so we must keep up our defenses with them. There are those with whom we will pursue deeper friendships or companionship when we leave the circle. And there are those with whom we may do battle when we leave.

"At this moment, however, we relinquish our selfish interests to a higher purpose. We are all equals here in the eyes of the higher order. Each one of us makes an equal contribution to the universe, but none of us is able to judge what that contribution is. The saint sitting across the wheel from the sinner must accept that the universe has created both of you. Fulfillment of your destiny lies not in understanding why that has come to be, each of us having such separate identities, but in accepting it as the truth for this moment.

"Have complete faith that the universe is complete only because of the unique contribution each one of us makes to it. We are not to judge ourselves. We are to see only that the universe is incomplete, in this moment, without the unique contribution of each person here in this circle, here on this planet at this time."

The important thing to note within this vision is that the individual "I" is fully acknowledged, even though a vision of something larger and more important (the universe) is also acknowledged. Moreover, the individual is not asked to give up his or her "I" in favor of a higher, or "right" position; on the contrary, he or she is asked to believe in it and to believe that in living out one's unique path he is fulfilling a purpose that is valuable in terms of the larger order. We are each like cells participating in the body of an animal; the larger organism's health depends on each cell maintaining its own individual integrity while simultaneously recognizing its interdependence within the whole.

At the Medicine Wheel, each participant may bring a question to be answered or a problem to be solved. He or she is said to *put the question into the center of the Wheel.* Then each person in the circle may comment on that problem, always answering as honestly as possible, clearly expressing any emotions aroused by the issues—feelings of anger, fear, denial, sympathy. They may also tell how they would solve the problem, or what another possible answer to the question might be.

In the end, the person who asked the question gets as many responses as there are people participating. And out of all these reflections—each one given in character with the respondent's unique Lens of Perception—the person sees that no single answer is correct for him or her—rather, it is the combined perceptions of the collective Lens created by the Wheel that leads one to the answer that is right for him. One comes away not only with the perspective that any single person's perceptions are, of necessity, incomplete, but perhaps more important, he comes away seeing that there is value in consulting the collection of Lenses provided by the Wheel.

JUNG'S EXPLORATION OF SHAMANISM AND THE LENS

C.G. Jung was intrigued by both the Oriental and shamanic religions, and during his lifetime he explored both in great depth. In the end, the vision of human consciousness that he articulated was much more in sympathy with shamanic than with Oriental thought. In the following paragraph, Jung reflects on the student of yoga, who seeks freedom from the "I," and tells why he favors embracing the "I," describing a position that the shaman would fully favor:

> He (the yoga student) wishes to free himself from nature; in keeping with this aim, he seeks in meditation the condition of image-lessness and emptiness. I, on the other hand, wish to persist in the state of lively contemplation of nature and of the psychic images. I want to be freed neither from human beings, nor from myself, nor from nature; for all these appear to me the greatest of miracles. Nature, the psyche, and life appear to me like divinity unfolded—and what more could I wish for? To me the supreme meaning of Being can consist only in the fact that it *is*...

Note the similarities between Jung's thinking and the vision of the Medicine wheel—that "Nature, the psyche, and life appear to me like divinity unfolded." He sees the individual "I," made possible by the Lens of Perception, as a manifestation of a higher order (divinity), just as the shaman does. And within this role the *psyche* (nearly interchangeable with my term, Lens of Perception) is merely one part of a whole to which we are inextricably bound.

Although Jung's work with human consciousness embraces the shamanic tradition, it is not always clear how aware he was of this alliance, although he did put considerable energy into studying it. One can only assume that on some level he acknowledged his debt to the shaman as well as to the yogin and Indian mystic. Throughout his writings, there are references to meetings with Indian gurus, students of the occult, Chinese philosophers, and Native Americans.

Jung's creative processes were much more shamanic than scientific. Exploring those processes provides us with some important models for accessing and making use of the inner resources of our Lens of Perception. For example, Jung claimed that one of the most important influences in his life was not another person or his alliance with the psychoanalytic movement, as one might suppose, but his association with spirit entities, which he recorded in his work *Septem Sermones ad Mortuos*. Jung said that he wrote this work in response to "the dead who addressed crucial questions to me." This is reminiscent of the Native American traditions of communicating with ancestral spirits whose beings appear to take form within the consciousness of the living.

Within the context of the Lens of Perception, it was in this Lens that Jung's dialogue with the dead took place. He described the process of writing the *Sermones* as one in which he asked questions and received answers with "figures in the unconscious," that is, on the Lens of Perception, not unlike what I described with my vision on the mountainside in Mexico. Jung claimed that it was out of this experience that all his life's work would follow.

Jung's description of one of his early explorations of the activities inside the Lens of Perception (psyche) might well have been out of shamanic literature, rather than out of the notebooks of one of the world's leading psychologists:

> There was a blue sky, like the sea, covered not by clouds but by flat brown clods of earth. It looked as if the clods were breaking apart and the blue water of the sea were becoming visible between them. But the water was the blue sky. Suddenly there appeared from the right a winged being sailing across the sky. I saw that it was an old man with the horns of a bull. He held a bunch of four keys, one of which he clutched as if he were about to open a lock. He had the wings of the kingfisher with its characteristic colors.

> During the days (that followed) I found in my garden, by the lake shore, a dead kingfisher! I was thunderstruck, for kingfishers are quite rare in the vicinity of Zurich and I have never since found a dead one. The body was recently dead—at the most, two or three days—and showed no external injuries.

Over the years, Jung developed an inner dialogue with the kingfisher, translating the creative insights that emerged from this activity into his exploration of the human psyche.

Because his work has a Western scientific foundation, Jung serves as a valuable resource, showing us a number of models for utilizing ancient traditions in contemporary life. In this task, Jung provides both the skepticism of the scientist and the curious, expansive nature of the mystic. What's more, his work with what I am calling the Lens was neither academic nor self-indulgent; rather, looking into the Lens, consciously participating in that inner world, he tapped resources as rich and varied as any available to him in the outer world.

It is easy, looking at the work of a man like Jung, to see the value of his individual Lens of Perception. His insights and experiences, recorded in literally thousands of pages of his writings, have influenced every generation that followed him. But sometimes, faced with intellectual giants like Jung, it is also easy to lose sight of the fact that everyone's unique vision, the activities within every person's Lens, also makes an important contribution, no matter how humble that contribution may seem to be.

THE LENS, THE GIFT

For most shamans, each person's Lens is seen as a gift from the universe. The universe provides the gift in order to complete a *whole* which none of us is able to grasp fully. At any given moment, that whole would be incomplete without the inclusion of every Lens that is in existence now or was ever in existence in the past. In this respect, the Lens is much more than the limiting factor many generations—especially those adhering to Oriental religious, and Western scientific belief systems—have perceived. Most have looked upon it as being comparable to blinders on a plough horse narrowing the animal's vision to that piece of the field the farmer wants him to till. And most have seen their goal as bieng one of removing the "blinders." In the following chapter, we'll be exploring quite a different perspective, that of recognizing the true purpose of the Lens and how, when it is embraced, it provides unique inner guidance for each person—a form of guidance that helps one consummate the responsibility inherent in receiving this gift from the universe.

FIFTH:

Hearing The Inner Voice—A Beacon Home

*"Yet are the humble free to hear the Voice
Which tells them what they are, and what
to do."*

—*A Course in Miracles*

The Lens of Perception can be compared to a highly sophisticated "homing device," or an "automatic pilot" on a ship or plane. It contains the *inner guidance* that is unique for each person, defining one's individuality and one's true purpose here on Earth. This inner guidance is important on two levels. First, it is important for the comfort of each individual—guiding career choices, choices of mates, where one is to live, what to eat, and so on. Second, it is important in terms of the health of the larger organization in which that individual takes part—family, community, nation, world, universe. In other words, the inner guidance is not unlike the genetic material that dictates how each cell will live its life both in the service of its individuality and in the service of the whole organism in which that individual is but one part.

Inner guidance finds expression in a variety of

ways. Sometimes it is the "inner voice;" sometimes it is a body feeling—a tightening in the stomach or jaw or back of the neck. Sometimes it is expressed as a "hunch" or a "funny feeling;" and sometimes it is a vision or dream whose message is very clear to the dreamer. These messages come in such a great variety of ways that it would be impossible to list them all here.

When heeded, messages of inner guidance keep us on our intended paths. When not heeded, we may stray far from our paths, resulting in discord, disease, poverty, confusion, depression, or a sense of not having a secure place in the world.

It goes even farther than that. Arnold Mindell is a Jungian therapist whose work with the "Dream Body" (roughly, the same as what we call the Lens of Perception) shows that there are links between our ability to follow the inner messages and our physical health. He says that "our dreams are world dreams," and the personal illnesses that result from not heeding the inner guidance provided by the dream body are more than personal issues: "no one is sick by himself, we all live in a field."

The Lens of Perception contains that part of us which we call inner guidance. But it contains many other things as well, some that help us focus more clearly on inner guidance, some that threaten to drown out the signals coming from it. Abraham Maslow calls it the "inner core." He compares it to the instincts of lower animals that direct their actions in nearly every moment of their lives. The inner core guides our lives much more gently and is much more flexible and responsive to the individual's volition or capacities for self determination than are the instincts of lower animals. But it is also the gift from that same universal source that provides the lower animals with their immutable instincts.

Maslow says that the messages of the inner core are:

> . . . weak, subtle and delicate, very easily drowned out by learning, by cultural expectations, by fear, by disapproval, etc. They are *hard* to know, rather than easy. Authentic selfhood can be defined in part as being able to hear these impulse-voices within oneself, i.e., to know what one really wants or doesn't want, what one is fit for and what one is *not* fit for, etc.

The Lens of Perception contains the inner core and all that we have built up around it. Some of what we have created or acquired obscures the messages of inner guidance. Some of what we have created or acquired intensifies those messages. And in a strange, contradictory way, some of the contents of the Lens direct our vision of life so that we emphasize—or even exaggerate—some aspects of it, while making it impossible for us to participate in others. An extreme example of this is the person whose perceptions are so bizarre that it is impossible for her to take part in everyday life and yet, as an outsider, her understanding of that life is filled with godlike accuracy. In Elizabethan drama, there was a traditional character who frequently illustrated this phenomenon. He was called the Fool, and was a person whose physical or mental deficiencies—insanity or blindness, for example—put him outside life as others knew it. As an "outsider," the Fool was able to observe the lives of those around him with a broader and deeper perspective than the people who were more actively engaged in it. The Fool could decipher the messages of inner guidance when others couldn't. Thus, the Fool in Shakespeare's *King Lear* could advise on the King's failure in learning to heed his inner voice: "Sirrah, thou should not have been old 'til thou had been wise!"

To one extent or another, every person suffers from the limited vision determined by the Lens. We would all like to be perfect human specimens, able to participate deeply in all that life has to offer, able to relate to and love all people, able to confront and easily solve any problem, unperturbed by what T.S. Eliot called "the little disturbances of man." But few have ever achieved such goals. We seem to require that filter which the Lens provides, and in requiring it we sacrifice the broader vision.

FOCUSING ON THE TRUE PATH

Henri Bergson contended that the human brain's function was not so much creative as it was eliminative. He believed that without the brain, the individual would be aware of all knowledge in the universe at all times. In this state of *direct knowing*, at every moment of one's life, the endless flow of information would render the person unable to act, unable even to concentrate on the moment, literally paralyzed by the endless flow of information.

The brain achieves this eliminative process through what we are here calling the Lens of Perception. The Lens is shaped from three key sources: (1) natural elements, including genetic influences such as skin color, eye color, physical size, aptitude, and even the fact that we are human beings rather than fish or apes or insects; (2) environmental elements, acquired very early in life, such as the parents we have or the siblings with whom we are raised, or early family blessings or crises, or the period of history into which we are born, over which most people cannot perceive themselves as having any choice; and finally, (3) opportunities and experiences chosen or created by the individual himself—education, the ability to interact voluntarily with others in the world, one's creative expressions, and so on.

As with a sophisticated camera, each Lens has a specific *field of vision* or *range of focus*. Depending on the Lens, some things in the picture will be in focus while others are not; some things will appear within the frame, some outside it. So also, your Lens of Perception will bring some things about the world into the light while leaving others in the dark, or outside the frame. The following story helps to illustrate how this works.

A DIVINE WARP IN THE LENS

An acquaintance of mine is the closest thing I have ever known to a modern-day saint. Her spiritual mission in life takes her into hospitals all over the world, where she counsels people with critical illnesses and offers strength to those who are dying. She lectures to huge audiences, and in all her work there is a message of caring and love that literally works miracles. Even in the middle of an auditorium packed with thousands who have come to hear her speak, you have the feeling that she is talking directly to you. You have the feeling that she truly cares about you, that she loves you unconditionally.

Alone with her, it is quite another matter. She always seems rushed. She appears to have no time for you. She asks your opinion about one subject or another, but when you start to give it, she interrupts to tell you something about herself. She fidgets nervously, and when you are speaking, she may even ask you to stop while she runs off to check a date on her calendar or leaves the room to make a phone call that she has forgotten.

The contradictions of this woman's personality are maddening to her friends and business associates. And yet, if you confront her with the fact that she is not paying attention to you, she will completely own up to it, apologizing for her rudeness in a way that you cannot deny. She finds one-on-one meetings painful unless they are completely focused on her mission. She can speak with a dying person, or to a crowd of thousands, bringing them healing comfort that surpasses anything I have ever witnessed. Yet, having lunch with a friend brings out her worst insecurities, and she falls back on defensive patterns of behavior that can leave everyone in her presence frustrated, bewildered, and even—if you don't know her well—insulted.

As one gets to know her, she confides that she struggles with her own ego all the time. She feels that she is terribly inadequate as a human being. Like a puppet whose strings she does not quite know how to control, her ego goes through its bizarre dance again and again, creating a painful experience of alienation from those whose attention she simultaneously loves and fears. Is she crazy? She would be the first to admit that she is, though she does not ask to be excused for her craziness. She has spent half her adult life in spiritual study, trying to make peace with her ego. Although she knows herself well, her successes in self-revelation still leave her a great distance from being comfortable with her life.

I mention her here because her life so clearly illustrates how that which we may perceive as a shortcoming, or a burden in our lives—in this case my friend's feelings of personal inadequacy—may not be a shortcoming after all, but may be a character trait providing the individual with a purpose far beyond what we ourselves can perceive. The cranky ego that seems to rule my friend's Lens of Perception, making close personal relationships so difficult for her, also seems to focus her mission, providing the world with a vision much larger than self-love. The great contradiction is that what some might perceive as her limitations are the root of a kind of expansiveness of character that allows her to succeed in a task where only a very few ever do. In this respect, that which some might perceive as handicaps or negative aspects of character may truly be gifts, essential roles that she is to fulfill in a whole that is much larger than we can perceive.

My friend, who brings so much comfort to millions of people the world over, is able to do that not because she is capable of being all things to all people, but because her particular Lens provides her with the vision for doing her particular task very well. From my own perspective, I would never choose to sacrifice the ability to enjoy close friendships in favor of having my friend's mission. But it may well be that this isn't a choice either one of us can make. Ultimately, the force that shapes our Lens is much greater than any of us.

TECHNIQUES FOR TURNING UP THE VOLUME

If it is true that the Lens contains both the inner voice and perceptions that obscure it, how can we get in touch with the messages that the inner voice would have us hear?

Maslow suggests that we use techniques such as those which Jung called "active imagination," that is, deliberately creating experiences in our minds that provide us with mirrors to explore the various facets of our inner selves. One example of this is the story I shared with you in the second chapter. The life experience of the vision on the mountain revealed to me that my fears—in that case manifested as a giant bird and as a mountain lion—are quite capable of distorting the truth. Furthermore, those animals were graphic representations of my deepest fears. And in getting to know those fears—and what they could do—I began to make peace with those elements of my being. In addition, it was in that vision that I was able to see the Lens clearly, and so begin to separate my own *creations* from the external world.

Another mirror for the inner world was when I asked you to imagine yourself standing on that mountain in Mexico with me, reflecting on where the experience took place for you. In doing so, you explored one part of your own inner world, the size and nature of your consciousness. Still another example of this mirroring of the inner self was the story about my saintly friend, in this chapter. With her story we explored how that which we perceive as personality problems may, at times, actually give impetus to a higher purpose or mission. In each case, the images produced in the stories allow you to explore your own feelings and insights, your perceptions about the way things *really* are.

You might also use divining systems, such as the *I Ching, Runes, Tarot,* or my own system which I call *Mind Jogger,* to start a process of "focused association" (free associations around a specific area of study) that helps you articulate your inner voice. In using divining systems of this kind, you use the cards or readings not as tellings of your fortune—a purpose for which they were never intended—but as highly sophisticated

"Rorschach" stimuli evoking ideas and images that are contained in the world of the Lens. For example, a person drawing a Tarot card of the Fool might reflect that there was a part of her, an impulse or a character of the inner world, that was able to move ahead in spite of adversity or fear. That person might find that drawing this card actually reminded her that she had this inner resource and could draw upon it for courage during challenging periods.

Another person drawing the same card might reflect that there was a part of him that plunged ahead without considering the consequences of his actions. Upon drawing this card in the process of making a major decision, he might be reminded to pay less attention to that part of himself until he had looked more carefully into the possible outcomes of a pending action. At the same time, that part of him might serve him well at the point that he did decide to act, impelling him forward with a sense of commitment that truly would be an asset.

Similarly, many books are available for using inner guides for learning how to amplify the inner messages expressed through dreams and visions. By learning to communicate with inner guides, you literally learn to communicate with the world inside your Lens. There are various speculations about the nature of these inner guides—ranging from seeing them as normal promptings within a person that get personified as "characters," just as they do in books, to seeing them as spiritual entities who offer their assistance in spiritual quests. Whatever the explanation, it is clear that these inner guides do connect us with sources of knowledge that transcend everyday thought. My own book, entitled *Inner Guides, Visions, Dreams, and Dr. Einstein* was written for this purpose of making these guides available to everyone.

THE OXYMORON

Emerson said, "With consistency a great soul has simply nothing to do...." Along these same lines, an important teacher of mine, Jerry Fletcher, contends that one of the greatest impediments to being fully in charge of our own inner resources is the fallacy that we must be "consistent of character." He believes that when we are most in touch with our inner voice, when our inner resources are flowing most strongly for us, we are not at all consistent. Instead, there is a kind of *dynamic tension* set up between our contradictions of character that seems to trigger the best in us. Dr. Fletcher uses oxymorons to show people how to identify that unique set of tensions within themselves and then translate those findings into constructive action.

By definition, an oxymoron is *the conjunction of paradoxical terms to make a specific point.* A popular joke that was making its rounds a few years ago said that "military intelligence" was an oxymoron, since the two words were mutually exclusive. In the case of my saintly friend in the story I just related to you, we would look at the two sides of her character: the Saint, on the one side; the alienated, lonely, ego-needy person on the other. Using the oxymoron principle, we might call her "The Haughty Saint," or perhaps "The Bashful Extrovert." Getting in touch and maintaining contact with her inner voice would not best be achieved by denying either side of her character but by recognizing and embracing them both, accepting the very real possibility that the part we are least approving of in ourselves is also what focuses the Lens to give the more acceptable side its power.

To explore this in yourself, simply write down three or more experiences you have had when you felt extremely good about something that you accomplished. When you do this, focus on the *quality of the experience for you*, that is, on feelings of self-satisfaction and self-pleasure, rather than on how important or unimportant others might have felt your accomplishment to be. And don't think you have to look for earth-shaking accomplishments. Events where you felt deeply satisfied with your own accomplishment can cover the gamut, from baking your first cake when you were nine years old to putting together a giant corporation in your forties.

After thinking about these experiences, consider your behavior around them. For example, were you pushy and selfish, even as you were open, encouraging, and friendly to others who were assisting you? If so, your oxymoron might be "The Humanistic Slave Driver." Or, you might discover that when you are at your best, you work secretively and in isolation for a period of time, then you bring your work into a group or team situation. The oxymoron to describe that dynamic might be "The Reclusive Team-Player," or "The Selfish Co-operator."

The oxymoron identifies contrasts of your character, delineating the polar points of your inner world. When they work really well, oxymorons reveal that there is an important relationship between what you may have considered to be your least virtuous traits and your very best. Oxymorons don't work for everyone. But when they do, they work like magic, helping them to accept those parts of their character that they find difficult to accept and, in the process, turning up the volume of their own inner voice.

THE PENDULUM

The *divining pendulum* is probably one of the oldest devices for reading messages from the inner self. The principle is very simple. In the study of psychoneurophysiology, we learn that the unconscious mind translates even the most deeply buried intuitive knowledge into minuscule muscular responses. No matter how good you think you are at self control, your inner experience will unconsciously be expressed in this way. By this same mechanism, a person who is good at reading faces can detect tiny muscular impulses—a tightening around an eyelid, a softening of the lip—in even the greatest master of the "poker face."

One way to detect these responses is with an electroencephalogram which records electrical impulses in the brain and nervous system. That technology is the basis for lie detectors. Few of us have access to such a machine, but we do have access to pendulums, which are a more primitive, but not necessarily less effective technology for achieving the same thing.

First, you need a pendulum. This may be a small pendant on the end of a delicate gold chain. Or, it may be as basic as a small lead weight like fishermen use, tied at the end of a line. The weight of the pendulum should not be much more than three to six ounces. The line to which the weight is attached should be highly flexible and no more than a foot in length.

Preparation: you will be asking your inner voice for assistance in making a decision that is important to you. This can be anything from what color to paint your bedroom to whether or not you should invest your life savings in an ice cream franchise.

Sit down in a comfortable chair where you can suspend the pendulum weight an inch or two above a table surface.

Take a deep breath. Let your body relax, your shoulders loose, your upper back and arm muscles soft.

Now, holding the pendulum above the table as steadily as you can without being rigid, think "Yes." Concentrate on "Yes." After a few moments, check the pendulum to see if it is going in a circle or back-and-forth. If there is no movement at all, it is probably because you are holding your arm too rigidly. Maybe you are resting your elbow on the table so tightly that tiny muscular impulses are being blocked. If this is happening, hold yourself more loosely and try again.

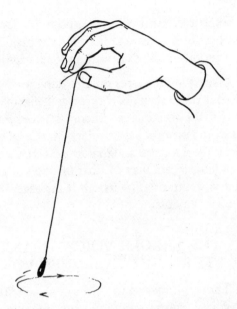

Now, repeating the same process, focus on "No." After a few moments take note of the pendulum's movement—is it circular or back-and-forth?

Check yourself several times until you feel that "Yes" is consistently one motion, and "No" is the other.

Now ask the pendulum a question with a simple yes or no answer. For example, ask, "Is my name Joe?"

Watch the pendulum to see what happens. Don't make any effort to move it or consciously influence its motion. If your name is Joe, it should move in the direction that it previously identified as "Yes." If your name is not Joe, it should move in the direction that it previously identified as "No."

Experiment with many questions that for you have simple yes or no answers. Then ask the pendulum your more serious questions, waiting for its response.

Like oxymorons, pendulums don't work for everyone. But when they do, they work like magic, helping you to make decisions consistent with your inner voice, and in the process helping confirm the fact that this voice is there for you and that its guidance can be trusted. Again, it is a way to turn up the volume of the inner voice, translating its subtle messages into detectable movements.

THE LARGER VOICE SPEAKING THROUGH THE INNER VOICE

Though it may sound like a contradiction, the inner voice originates from a source outside us. There are many names for this source: God, Mother Earth, The Noosphere, the "collective unconscious," Universal Spirit, and so on. Depending on the Lens of Perception belonging to the person describing this source, that source may be seen in religious terms or not. One of the most universally acceptable descriptions of this source comes from John The Evangelist, who begins his Testament with the following:

When all things began, the Word already was. The Word dwelt with God, and what God was, the Word was. The Word, then, was with God at the beginning, and through him all things came to be; no single thing was created without him. All that came to be was alive with life, and that life was the light of men.

Theologians call the Word described here the Logos. German theologian Georg Kuhlewind states that the Logos is the spirit of Creation, the Word of God out of which All was made. As parts of the Creation itself, each one of us is also a single, though minuscule, manifestation of the Logos. Kuhlewind says, "the Logos is present in everyone, and man cannot find his own reality alone."

A number of years ago, I was interested to learn that the Hopi Indians believe that everyone comes into life with a "Starting Place." For them, the Starting Place represents inner guidance or inner resources that are God-given and that guide individuals throughout their lives. In modern terms it includes aptitudes—one's gift for doing a particular thing in life. Beyond that it includes the ability to perceive the external world in a particular way, for one person to be attracted to blue while another is attracted to red, and for one to be attracted to a high energy life style while another is attracted to a quiet, monastic way of life. In short, it constitutes what we've been calling the Lens of Perception.

The Logos is expressed and made manifest through all of creation, but not through any single element within it. Where humankind is concerned, Logos is expressed through the 3.2 billion individuals who populate the Earth. The particular individuality of each Lens is as essential to the total expression of Logos as are the particular individualities of the cells that make the totality of your body possible. Remember that in any living organism, each cell has a specific assignment—a duty to perform, a specific shape, and a determined location to fulfill. The same might be said for you and the path you must follow to fulfill your life's purpose as a manifestation of the Logos.

In the following chapter we explore some of the ways we may see the Lens of Perception to set up clearer channels of communication with the Logos.

SIXTH:

Joining Inner And Outer Communities

> *"Everything in Nature contains all the powers of Nature. Everything is made of one hidden stuff."*
>
> —*Emerson*

In the mid-sixties, I spent a number of years in the work apprentice program at "The San Francisco Actors Workshop," then the leading avant-garde theater on the West Coast. At the same time, I was also associated with a peyote shaman, who taught his own brand of "inner theater," a fact that no doubt colored my perceptions during that period of my education.

The teachings I came away with, as a result of these combined experiences, centered on a vision that the Lens is our own inner theater, a sort of teaching theater that is always with us and which has an unlimited cast of players. In another way, it is as though this inner world—which all of us have—is our first family, or community. We belong to it before we belong to any other. It is here that our primary loyalties lie. And this alliance will move us into alliances with other individuals, families, and communities in the external world, and even extended into the Logos, that will help us carry out the higher purposes of our lives.

The interactions we have with those members of our inner community draw us to some people and repel us from others in the outer world, just as friends in our outer worlds draw us into friendships with ever-increasing numbers of their friends and acquaintances. If we do not take the time to learn the lessons of the inner theater, or are not well-acquainted with that inner community, we may never come to know those who would love, teach, and support us in the outer world. (Without "introductions" that come about through our knowledge of ourselves, through the inner world—I call the process "Intrapersonal Communication"—our greatest allies, both there and in the outer world, may always appear as strangers to us, and we may consequently overlook those who would be most important to our personal growth.

COMMUNICATIONS WITH INNER HELPERS

In his exploration of the inner world Jung showed how certain promptings within that world—he called it the "unconscious"—often took on separate identities of their own. Parts of himself appeared as characters—men, women, and children, who seemed to be playing out important themes, relevant to his life. He stated further that their apparent autonomy "is a most uncomfortable thing to reconcile oneself to, and yet the very fact that the unconscious presents itself in that way gives us the best means of handling it."

Jung established ways of communicating with the inner world, starting with fully acknowledging the characters within—indeed, by acknowledging that whole world that lived within him. After permitting the inner people to have their separate identities, he would speak with them, as you might speak with a friend sitting next to you in your living room. In this way, he became familiar with what they wanted. If they seemed to want something from the outer world that was disagreeable to him, Jung was free to refuse them their wants. But more often than not, they provided him with knowledge that improved the quality of his life and gave all who followed him broad insights into the nature of the human consciousness.

C.G. Jung had an inner guide who he called Philemon, who "for me represented superior insight" (Jung's quote), that is, knowledge beyond the ego. Jung said of Philemon: "I went walking up and down the garden with him, and to me he was what the Indians called a guru."

More than fifteen years after his introduction to Philemon, Jung met a friend of Gandhi's, and spoke to him about the Indian's education. The man told Jung that his spiritual teacher had been Shankaracharya. Jung knew of a great Indian teacher by that name, but that teacher had been dead for centuries. He asked if this had been the same person.

"Yes, I mean him," the man told Jung.

93

"Then you are referring to a spirit?" Jung asked.

"Of course it was his spirit," the man replied. "There are ghostly gurus too. Most people have living gurus. But there are always some who have a spirit for a teacher."

The Northern Cheyenne shaman Hyemeyohsts Storm also speaks of the importance of recognizing beings who exist in your inner world. Here he reflects on his own peoples' process of working with the Lens:

> . . .within every man there is the Reflection of a Woman, and within every woman there is the Reflection of a Man. Within every man and woman there is also the Reflection of an Old Man, an Old Woman, a Little Boy, and a Little Girl.

Storm says further that:

> Often our first Teacher is our own heart. This Teaching Voice is spoken of by the old Sun Dance Teachers as the Chief.

MOLECULAR AND SPIRITUAL COMMUNICATION

We know that in advanced physics, reality is inevitably altered by the presence of the observer. The billions of electrons that make up the observer himself interact with electrons that make up the thing being observed, changing its structure. In the words of physicist Ludwig Boltzmann:

> My observation has not only recorded reality. I am much more than an objective observer, since my presence, the presence of the particles that make up my very being, alters that reality.

French physicist Jean Charon has stated that the interactions of those same particles, more specifically, the electrons, constitute what religious thinkers have described as the world of Spirit. This, of course, includes the billions of electrons that we each carry around as our selves. Because our physical beings, as well as our thoughts and feelings, are made possible by interactions between electrons both inside and outside our physical boundaries, we theoretically are in communion at all times with the universe and with the Logos. The Lens of Perception, highly charged with electrons that store our personal history, plays a very great part indeed, constantly interacting with that which we observe, and constantly changing it.

On the one hand, we accept the possibility that electrons buzzing about in our consciousness can affect the physical world beyond the boundaries of our skin. But the implications go further than that. Each person is also the receiver of those buzzings—you of my buzzing, me of yours. If your buzzing electrons can affect the physical world, does it not follow that those same buzzings can affect me, since both my consciousness and my physical body are made up of material that is responsive to the electrons—indeed, I am electrons myself. It is at this point that psychology, spiritual questions, and physics truly merge, asking us to take a quantum leap in our thinking.

Ludwig Boltzmann tells us:

> Only when one admits that spirit and will are not something over and above the body, but rather complicated actions of material parts whose ability so to act becomes increasingly perfected by development, only when one admits that intuition, will and self-consciousness are merely the highest stages of development of these physiochemical forces of matter by which primeval protoplasmic bubbles were enabled to seek regions that were more favorable and avoid those that were less favorable for them, only then does everything become clear in psychology.

DANCING THE LOGOS

During the time that I was involved in the theater, I became particularly interested in dances and dramatic performances in which both performers and audience were transported beyond the borders of their egos into paranormal consciousness states. Typically, performers donned ceremonial garb and masks to depict gods, goddesses, animal entities, and various forces in nature that played important roles in their mythology. Dancing to steady, monotonous rhythms—sometimes influenced by hallucinogenics—the actors assumed the characters of these entities. In the pro-

cess, the dancer was released from his own ego, and ←
for a time took on another identity.

By assuming other characters and then surrender-
ing to them, one gained access to knowledge they might
otherwise not have been able to access. With ego sus-
pended, everyday perceptions dissolved, the players became open to the "Universal Truths," or to that which
the biblical scholars call "The Logos."

Bible

It is my belief that through observing the theater
within the Lens of Perception, and through participating in that inner community of which that theater is
a part, we not only gain a greater understanding of our
individual lives, and our life purposes, we gain access
to the universal knowledge described above. The trance
dances in the external world can be effective in this
for some people—performers and spectators alike—
because they mimic a process that is already going on
inside each one of us.

The success of the individual as a participant in
the Logos is dependent on a kind of peace and har-
mony established between the inner world and the
outer one. If we are to prosper, if we are to enjoy satisfying relationships, if we are to enjoy the very best in
ourselves, we must not avoid the inner world. Not
everyone need do that consciously or deliberately, of
course. There are, after all, many fully happy, successful, and spiritually evolved people who are not in the
least aware of the process I'm describing, but who
nevertheless are able to embrace the inner world and
join it with the most positive influences in the exter-

nal world. Part of their success may be luck, part of it may be that they practice some of the processes I describe without knowing it.

The study of the Lens of Perception is only one way of getting what you need from your inner world. There are many others, and many teachers now available. This seems to be a time when information of this kind is being made widely available, and usually without the long initiation processes that are associated with the traditions out of which they come.

Until the past two decades, techniques for getting to know the inner world, and for traveling safely within it, have been in the hands of an elite—the priest, the Oracle, the guru, the shaman, and more recently, the psychologist. But now we are living in a time of rapid change, a time when greater and greater numbers of people are asking for information and tools to expand their understanding and mastery of their own inner worlds. In the Reformation of the sixteenth century, mankind claimed and won the right to *private judgment* in interpreting the Bible. Now the struggle is more quiet and more subtle, without violence, and often without public fanfare, but no less important than what happened 400 years ago. As Marilyn Ferguson has pointed out in her book *The Aquarian Conspiracy*, it is a revolution "whose roots are old and deep in human history, (and which) belongs to all of us."

We are claiming and winning our rights to private judgments about our own inner worlds. Progress is being made, in part, because of an important demystification which is occuring. Superstitions about the inner world and self-power—many of which were designed to make us fearful and thus keep the mastery of these domains in the hands of the high priests and priestesses—are being dissolved. In the past decade there has been a significant change in the nature of the knowledge that is making its way to the public. We are no longer satisfied with *only* hearing about other peoples' journeys into the inner world, as in the work of Carlos Castaneda and others. Instead, we are asking for and getting the "maps" and "navigational tools" for making these journeys ourselves. Moreover, the new movement is away from viewing the inner world journeys as forms of exotica, finding instead that our journeys inward can vastly improve the quality of our daily lives, in everything from relationships to spiritual growth to business careers.

Historically, we have just passed an important turning point, taking the study of the inner world out of the occult. I think of it as a stage of growth similar to what happened immediately after the discovery of the Americas 500 years ago. In the beginning, any information about the newly discovered continent was viewed by the Europeans as exotic and unfathomable. Most people could not imagine themselves going there. A few brave souls saw it as a rich opportunity. Then, as people emigrated to the new continent, exotic perspectives gave way to pragmatics. We learned what the opportunities and problems of the new territory were and began to apply ourselves accordingly.

At the risk of becoming too metaphorical, in the past few years we have seen *mass migrations to the inner world*. More and more people are becoming familiar with the territory, and as they do, their interests have moved from exotics to pragmatics. What might once have been looked upon as *occult insight* is now being translated into real-world application, helping us in our personal relationships, our careers, and in the day-to-day living of our lives. Meditating, communicating with inner guides, making use of synchronicity, and the systematic use of what were once known as "intuitive" or "psychic" abilities are all becoming daily skills applied to everyday issues.

Emerson spoke of "the voices which we hear in solitude" which sadly "grow faint and inaudible as we enter into the world." He spoke of these voices as the true source of each person, guiding him or her in the path intended by God. Each person's true power was to be recognized by the awakening and expression of that voice in the world: "The power which resides in him is new in nature, and none but he knows what that is which he can do, nor does he know until he has tried." It is in the service of these goals that our renewed interest in the inner world is being directed, since it is through the skills and insights unfolding here that the voice within gains the strength required to meet both the personal and global challenges before us.

THE WORKBOOK:

Applying Your Knowledge Of The Lens Of Perception

After getting to know the Lens of Perception, and after consciously experiencing how it works in your life, a number of new possibilities present themselves. The first is that you can get a sense of your own self-power by observing how your inner world, the Lens of Perception, actually affects the outer world and brings about changes there. Through guided meditations in this section of the book, you will actually discover concrete evidence—evidence that you can see and touch in the world around you—showing you that this is true. This exercise will help you focus on the four facets of your individuality: (1) your own self-worth; (2) your ability to distort the truth; (3) your value in the context of the Logos or Source; and (4) the real source of your self-power.

Your knowledge of the Lens will also serve you in the area of personal relationships. Here you will learn a meditation technique to help you see how conflicts can be dissolved through the Lens, not by one person giving in to another, and not by one person attempting to make changes to be more like the other, but by embracing your own Lens, which defines your individual identity, and recognizing the wisdom of allowing the other person to embrace his or hers. In doing this you "embrace rather than erase" your differences, and adversaries join each other in the common bond of knowing that it is partially through expressing our individual differences that we fulfill the gift provided us by the Logos, or Source.

One of the most valuable things that becomes accessible through your knowledge of the Lens is the conscious and deliberate skill of "manifesting," or *getting what you want from life*. Most of us are acquainted with people who appear to go after and get whatever they want, with relative ease. They are clear about the jobs they want, the kinds of relationships they desire, the education they wish to pursue, where they want to live, and their general lifestyle. And for all intents and purposes they appear to draw to themselves everything they want, fulfilling their wishes as if by magic. Others of us struggle, and are not always clear about what we want, and even when we do decide what we want, getting it does not come easily. We appear to be *chasing after* what we want, rather than *attracting what we want to us*. The difference is found in manifesting skills—which some people come by naturally and others must take great pains to learn.

In this section of the book, I will be describing one technique for getting what you want from life that is highly effective for most people. It is one that takes full advantage of the power of the Lens of Perception to shape your life into experiences where you fully enjoy personal fulfillment.

MOVIES OF THE MIND

Some of the processes I'll be describing for working with the Lens depend on your ability to create a kind of living movie inside your Lens. Now that you're aware of how the Lens works, with our inner world shaping our experiences of the external world, the principle here is quite simple. In everyday life, the world inside the Lens is created through a combination of external stimuli and that which is contained by our Lens. If you create a new element in that Lens—a person, an experience, a concept—all experience after that point will be changed. Any new elements you may introduce, through pure serendipity or your own efforts, will change the inner world, and thus will change how you experience the external world.

Positive thinking, made popular by proponents such as Norman Vincent Peale, made use of the Lens of Perception, though not by name. Peale said that by changing our perceptions of ourselves from "have nots" to "haves" we could get more out of life. And he was right. His techniques not only *inspired* millions of people, they *changed people's perceptions* of themselves, and truly did win them greater success in their lives.

But the process for getting what we want from life has become even more sophisticated than that. Modern science has entered the picture, and in the work of researchers such as Carl Pribram and Roger Sperry, we have been able to create a much more complete picture of human consciousness than was ever before available to us. We have learned, for example, that we possess what appears to be two brains, rather than one. The left brain specializes in logical and linear matters, such as mathematics and language. The right brain specializes in more three-dimensional or "spatial" processes, such as artistic and movement oriented processes.

The two brains rarely work completely independent of one another. On an organic level, they are connected by a dense mass of nerve tissue called the *corpus callosum*, which constitutes a highly sophisticated communication system between the two sides of the brain. All of this is important in the study of human consciousness and the Lens of Perception only in that it gives us guidelines for designing techniques for utilizing the Lens more consciously. Specifically, we know that it is possible to activate the imagination and to create experiences in the mind that will affect the quality of our lives in the external world.

A number of years ago, Elmer and Allyce Green, through a research grant provided by the Menninger Clinic, collected scientifically measured data concerning techniques used by shamans, yogins, and Indian mystics. They discovered, among other things, that the "human consciousness does not distinguish between that which is real and that which is imagined." How does this affect us in our everyday lives? This question is best answered by looking at two examples of how negative belief systems can translate into life-threatening physiological conditions.

The most dramatic example I can offer is in the practice of "Voodoo," in which the unwavering belief that the Voodoo doctor's spell on you is fatal does in fact bring about physiological changes in the person's body that might be equated to severe emotional shock, which can lead to death. In modern life, a similar mechanism is at work when one partner in a lifelong relationship dies, leaving the other alone in their old age. Although there may be no physiological reason that the survivor cannot get along on their own, their grief and their firm belief that they cannot live without their partner actually causes glandular and neurological changes that hasten their death.

The same mechanism of beliefs affecting our physiological well being can be used in a positive way. In the early 1960s, Carl Simonton, a radiologist specializing in cancer treatment, discovered that belief systems appeared to affect recovery rates for people with cancer. Those who felt powerless against the disease, and who felt that they were complete victims, did in fact succumb, while people with the same medical prognosis but with a firm belief that they had the power to fight the disease, had a significantly higher cure rate.

Simonton combined standard cancer treatment, such as surgery, radiology, and chemotherapy, with mental exercises aimed at helping people to adopt new beliefs in their ability to fight disease and heal themselves, to replace old beliefs of victimization and helplessness. The results proved promising, with his patients showing a better cure rate than similar patients receiving only standard treatment.

In more recent years, sports performance psychologists have learned that the most successful and accomplished athletes utilize a process called "mental rehearsal" to prepare themselves for physical challenge. For example, world class athletes such as O.J. Simpson and Arnold Palmer have said that they create detailed mental pictures of themselves performing with great success. These mental pictures, research has shown, go much further than *positive thinking*.

Whereas positive thinking merely sets up an expectation of success, boosting the morale of the athlete, mental rehearsal prepares the central nervous system in the co-ordination of muscle tissue and nerve fiber. Those mental images created in the rehearsal are triggered at the moment of actual play, and like a highly sophisticated computer program, they send out signals that cause nerve cells to fire and muscles to contract or relax according to the rehearsed plan. To use a computer term, mental rehearsal is like writing the *software program* that directs the complex operations of performing a particular physical feat.

How does mental rehearsal fit in here? The answer becomes obvious when we see that this process takes place inside the Lens of Perception. Within his or her Lens the athlete creates a playing field, or gymnasium, or golf course, or tennis court, complete with players, obstacles, and whatever else he or she might encounter in real life. And that rehearsal in the Lens is as important to the mind and central nervous system as the physical rehearsal is to the development of muscle and physical stamina.

Imaginary rehearsals of any event in our lives will affect the world within the Lens of Perception, either positively or negatively, just as real experiences in everyday life will. We are only now discovering the extraordinarily positive effect that imagined experience can have in our lives, giving us a choice about the kinds of "programs" that dominate our Lens and which affect our relationship to the external world.

The process for voluntarily introducing new material to the Lens—be it for an athletic performance, for achieving success in your job, or for an improved personal relationship—is quite simple. It consists of first preparing the brain to be open and receptive and then introducing previously prepared imaginary experiences. There is no great mystery about how this process works: The brain's receptivity is optimal when you are in a physically relaxed state. And in that receptive state, an imagined experience you introduce is quickly integrated into the inner world of the Lens. The receptive state is achieved by grounding and relaxing techniques which most people familiar with meditation will have already experienced.

COMPLETION THROUGH REAL WORLD ACTION

No matter how complete an imagined experience may be, the person must still bring that perception into play in the real world. This is done by taking action. Arnold Palmer may create the most beautiful mental rehearsal of teeing off from the first green, but the ball will never get off the ground unless he translates that

Six Key Principles of The Lens of Perception

The six basic premises upon which this workbook is based are as follows:

1. The Lens is a normal and inescapable part of the *human* experience. This is one aspect of our lives that we share with all people and which makes us One.

2. An important part of the Lens is the inner guidance or inner core that directs us on a path of self-fulfillment through fulfillment of our purpose in the Logos. This also is an aspect of our individual lives that we share with all others and that makes us One.

3. Inner guidance is often obscured by perceptions within the Lens, and clearing the way to receive the inner guidance is the key task for achieving self-power. The process for doing this is unique for each person. There are no *force fits* in this process; if the inner guidance must be pushed aside in order to fit in, the fit simply isn't right. Though each person must find his or her own path in this, the need for that lonely search is shared with all people, and makes us One.

4. The Lens and inner guidance focuses our vision, allowing us to give our best attention to interests and activities that fulfill our true path.

5. There is a built-in contradiction to all of the above. Differences in the contents of the Lens, and the boundaries set up by these differences, can lead to conflicts between people, misunderstandings, and impatience. This fact of the human condition is also shared with all others, and makes us One.

6. Mankind is One. We are One through our identification with the Logos, or Source of All. We are One through our sharing a common contradiction, wherein the Lens of Perception defines individual boundaries that are both the source of our loneliness and the source of our union with the Logos.

Purpose:

The purpose of this exercise is to create a sense of feeling grounded, relaxed, secure and oriented with the immediate physical surroundings. This experience is essential for most of the exercises in this section of the book. It is especially important during that part of the manifesting exercise where you are making "mental movies." In making these mental movies, there is a tendency to experience a "floating" sensation, which some people describe as "leaving the body." We are, of course, not literally leaving the body at such times; however, when one focuses so much attention on the inner world, there is a tendency to lose touch temporarily with normal physical sensations and to feel disoriented. The Triangulation Exercise allows you to experience deeply the mental movies, or the meditations I describe, with a minimum of discomfort in returning to a normal state of consciousness. This exercise is, in itself, a basic meditation that will help you clear distracting influences from your Lens of Perception during times when you are under stress or feeling pressure. In addition, it can provide you with the simple pleasure of a moment of relaxation in the middle of a busy day.

You may wish to have a friend read the following to you as you do the actual exercise. If that is not possible, record it on a cassette recorder and play it back for yourself as you do the exercise. Read slowly, with appropriate pauses so that you can have plenty of time to respond to each step of the instructions.

Preliminaries:

Begin by giving yourself permission to devote the next ten minutes to yourself, without having to respond to other people or to distractions such as the telephone. If there is a telephone in the room unplug it, confident that if there is an urgent call, the caller will get back to you when you are done.

Instructions:

Sit in a comfortable chair, preferably one with a straight back so that you can maintain a relaxed but alert state.

Let your hands rest easily in your lap.

Let your face be relaxed and soft, jaw slack, eyes closed.

Take a deep breath, slowly letting your chest and abdomen fill up. Hold it briefly, then exhale through your nose. Slowly. Easily.

Take two or three more breaths, each time exhaling slowly and easily.

Breathe normally.

Imagine that you are sending out thin silver threads, or thin beams of light, like laser beams, to the eight corners of the room—the four corners of the ceiling and the four corners of the floor. Imagine that these threads or light beams extend from your navel to these eight points.

Imagine a thread or light beam going from your navel, down through the floor to the center of the Earth.

Now recall some place in the world, perhaps a room in your home, or a place you used to go as a child, or perhaps a vacation spot, where you feel secure, happy, completely at ease with yourself. Imagine a thread or light beam going from your navel to that place, connecting you with it at this time.

For a moment, let your attention be focused on the lines you have established between your navel and these ten positions: The eight corners of the room where you are sitting; the thread or light beam to the center of the Earth; the thread or light beam to the place where you feel secure, happy, completely at ease with yourself.

Sit and enjoy this experience for as long as you wish.

When you are ready to leave the experience, take a deep breath, exhale, and open your eyes.

Look around you. Check out each of the four corners of the ceiling and each of the four corners of the floor.

Move your feet so that you feel the floor solidly under your soles.

Stretch your arms high above your head, then as far as you can reach out to your sides.

Get up slowly. Move around, giving yourself permission to take a few moments to enjoy lingering feelings of relaxation and pleasure that you may still feel.

CLOSING NOTES

Most relaxation and orienting exercises require several repetitions, preferably over a number of days, before you begin to fully enjoy the benefits. I recommend that you do this exercise every other day for a week, allowing one day of rest in between your practice sessions.

You want to integrate this exercise fully into the world of your Lens of Perception. You will know this has happened when you can get the full benefits simply by closing your eyes and thinking about the exercise. It will all happen automatically, and your sense of being oriented and relaxed will then be as accessible as any other important experience in your life.

EXERCISE #2:

Observing Your Own Power

Purpose:

The purpose of this exercise is to allow you to experience how your Lens of Perception affects the physical world. You will see that you cause changes to occur in the external world through the images you hold in your Lens. It is useful to do this exercise as an affirmation, demonstrating how your presence in the world really does make a difference, a difference that we often don't see for ourselves.

Preliminaries:

This exercise should be done while sitting at home, preferably in a place where you feel completely at ease, and where you are surrounded by at least a few of your favorite objects.

Begin this exercise by relaxing and orienting yourself. The Triangulation exercise is excellent for this.

Instructions:

Look around you and take the time to study carefully everything you see. Let your eyes wander over the surfaces of things. Enjoy the colors and textures of the things you see. If you feel drawn to picking things up and touching them, do that. If taste or smell are involved, do that. Take thorough pleasure in everything around you.

Now close your eyes and pretend that all these things exist *only* in your Lens. Let yourself enjoy them as they exist in your inner world; do this by remembering the experience you had only moments before as you really did touch or smell or look at these things.

Say to yourself, "I have created all this. I have brought these things into my life, and I have created the pleasure I experience in them."

At first, this statement may seem unbelievable or absurd. After all, you have not shaped the wood and assembled that chair across the room. You have not shorn the wool and woven the fabric for the upholstery on the couch where you are lounging. How then could you have created all this?

The point is that you have probably not created the objects you see around you. However, the experience of those objects is your creation. And chances are, the objects that you enjoy in this rom would not have been present in this place had it not been for your involvement with them. It does not matter if the objects you are enjoying were given to you by friends, or if you purchased them yourself, or even if, by chance, you did make them yourself. This space where you are sitting would not have been possible without you. You are the key organizer whether you did that organization consciously or not.

Notice as you look at your experience of this place, or as you enjoy these objects in your own Lens, that this is one little piece of the world that would be quite different had it not been for you. Your presence in the world has made this possible. Something *similar* could have occupied this space without you—but it would not have been the *same* as it is now.

You are the difference!

Think about something you have created or accomplished, either on your own or with other people. In the inner world of your Lens, explore that creation or accomplishment in depth. Recall a few of the specific actions you took in the process of achieving this thing. As much as you can, remember how you felt at those times. Simply note these feelings.

Recall the earliest part of the project you can. Try to go back to the time when it was nothing more than an idea in your mind. Or perhaps, instead of an idea, you had the feeling that you would like to take part in the thing you accomplished. Focus your attention on that idea or feeling for a moment. Realize as you do this that your part in the final accomplishment began as this seed idea or feeling experienced by you only in the Lens. Without this early experience in your Lens, and the action you took as a result of it, the final outcome would never have been possible.

Others may have been able to do similar things, but you made the difference here. Your Lens of Perception—and the actions you took as a result—made this particular accomplishment possible.

You make the difference!

Think about a relationship you have with one other person. Let yourself recall a time when the two of you shared a moment of great pleasure and satisfaction. Try to recall what you were thinking and feeling at that moment. What were you experiencing within your Lens? Note, as you do, that what you held in your Lens made your pleasure in this moment possible, a pleasure amplified by your friend's experience of your pleasure.

You make the difference!

Recall as many significant experiences of your life as you wish. Note how you felt, your earliest involvements with the experience, and note how you contributed to those experiences through your Lens of Perception—by being motivated to participate directly, by being present in a way that brought pleasure, encouragement, or support to others, or by offering your inner resources in a way that supported or helped change a situation for the better. Note the importance of your inner world, your Lens, in all these experiences. And note that only you possess that Lens, making your involvement unique.

You make the difference!

CLOSING THOUGHTS

This directed meditation is subtle. You may not immediately feel any dramatic results. But each time you do it, your awareness of the power you possess through your Lens will increase. As it does, you will have a natural tendency to value your own contribution in the world more, and to count the world of your Lens as a major resource in every situation where you might choose to involve yourself.

When you are doing the Manifestation exercise, the self-affirmations which you receive through Observing Your Own Power will be especially important. Seeing that your Lens really does affect the external world, you will be much more motivated, and have faith based on evidence, which sets the stage for highly successful Manifestations of new pleasures and achievements.

Personal Conflict And Healing: Developing The Power Of Positive Detachment

Purpose:

The purpose of this exercise is to find calm solutions to difficult personal conflicts. It helps you develop skills for stepping back and taking a closer look—not only at the situation but at your own Lens of Perception. Even in those situations where satisfactory solutions cannot be found immediately, the skills presented here allow you to leave frustrating or maddening situations with a sense of self-control and a deeper, highly satisfying understanding of your own inner world.

When confronted with interpersonal conflicts in the real world of family relationships, friendships, or business, all too many theories, which look good on paper, go out the window. The failure of many spiritual and psychological systems for resolving conflict is that in order to work well, everyone involved must agree upon the basic goals of the system. That, of course, is only rarely feasible. However, in the exercise that follows, it is assumed that the person with whom you are in conflict hasn't the vaguest awareness of this book or the concept of the Lens of Perception. There need be no agreement between you and them.

Preliminaries:

Real conflicts in the real world need real attention. If, for example, there is a person vying for your position at your job, and misusing you in order to achieve his own ends, that fact will clearly cause you concern, creating pressure that you can't ignore. In most problems of this kind, there are several alternatives open to you: (1) You may choose to meet this person head on, and confront him openly with what you feel he is doing to you; (2) you may choose to withdraw from the battle, let him have his way, and move on to another job; (3) you may seek outside help from a friend, consultant, or supervisor; (4) you may choose to do nothing, allowing the other person to do what he wishes, regardless of the expense to you; (5) you may choose to do the following exercise and combine the results with any of the above.

The skills described here are not, of course, limited to conflicts at work. In married life they will be helpful in reducing tensions between mates. In friendship they will be helpful in softening the edge of personal differences. Everywhere, the skills will help reduce the tension you feel between the time you are first confronted with it and the eventual solution.

If you find yourself dwelling on the problem at times when there is really no constructive action you can take to change things, use this time instead for the following exercise.

You may wish to use a notebook or tape recorder

for the following. Read the exercise through all the way before you start.

Instructions:

Give yourself permission to adopt the belief that the person or problem with which you are confronted right now has become a part of your inner world for a purpose that will ultimately benefit you— regardless of the more immediate outcome you presently imagine. Even though there is a real person in the outer world with whom you are having this trouble, pretend for now that all you have to deal with is the person or the problem in your Lens of Perception.

Bring the person or problem to the forefront of your inner world. Picture him, her, or it in your Lens. Allow yourself to experience that picture. Name the emotions you are feeling: perhaps anger, frustration, bewilderment, pain, anxiety, dismay, or helplessness.

Now, in your imagination (and not in real life) tell the person you are seeing in your Lens the following:

"You are here within my Lens of Perception. You are, at this moment of solitude, my own creation. You will remain here only as long as I wish you to be here."

Pause. Let yourself get used to this idea. Realize that in order to experience yourself engaged in some way with the real person in the external world, it is necessary to create that person within your Lens, to provide them with an identity in your inner world.

In other words, that person has both an external reality and the inner reality you create in your Lens.
Stay very clear about the idea that it is with the inner reality that you are presently dealing. There are a number of ways to maintain that focus. For example, you might imagine this person surrounded by a glass cage, or that any communication between you must be done over an intercom or a telephone. It is your inner world; you can have it any way you wish. Put this person in another town, hundreds of miles away, if that makes you feel comfortable. And realize that regardless of this distance, you can still see them and communicate with them easily.

Begin a dialogue with this person. You may speak aloud, or you may wish only to *think* about what you would like to tell them. Start with a very positive statement, pointing you in the direction of what would be a happy outcome for you. Here's an example:

"At present, when I bring you into my Lens, I feel angry and out of control. I would like to bring you into my Lens and feel calm and in charge of myself."

Wait for a moment, until you can hold that person in your Lens and feel calm. If your calmness does not come in a few moments, remind yourself that the person you have created in your Lens is, at this time, completely your own creation. They have no power over you except what you are willing to give them. Your experiences at this moment belong only to you.

Go on to ask the person you perceive in your Lens anything that comes to your mind, allowing an imaginary conversation to begin between you and them. Here are a few samples:

- *"What are you doing in my inner world? What purpose do you serve?"*

- *"Are there any other people like you in my inner world?"* (If the answer is yes, try putting them together and imagining how they would interact.)

- *"If you were a teacher or guru, how would you communicate your lesson to me in plain language, rather than in the way you are now doing?"*

- *"What are you trying to learn from your association with me? And, if I were your teacher, how would I teach the same lesson to you in plain language?"*

Choose one of the above questions, or invent your own, to get a dialogue started. Then pause and wait for an answer. This answer may come in a variety of ways. You may have the experience of that person talking directly to you. You may feel answers coming from the person as though telepathically, or you may have thoughts and feelings that clearly come from your own mind. However this communication takes place for you is okay. It can be helpful to write down or tape record your conversations.

It is often helpful to play back the tape you have made, or read what you've written, after some time has passed. Be in a meditative state when you do this. Starting the reflective session with the Triangulation Exercise can be extremely helpful.

If you don't get any surprising results right away, don't be discouraged. Keep in mind that you have lived most of your life in a society that discourages communication with the inner world. As Emerson said, over 100 years ago: "Society is in conspiracy against the manhood of every one of its members." Every time you do this exercise, you are affirming the importance of the inner world in your life, and through doing so, communication will become easier and easier.

Although it may seem like a strange contradiction, it is often from those we perceive as our greatest adversaries that we learn the most. The intensity felt—either positive or negative—is often a measure of the depth and benefit of the final message.

CLOSING THOUGHTS

There is always a difference between the perception in the Lens and external reality. The person with whom you converse in your inner world is not the same as the person challenging you in the external world. Usually, resolutions with people in the external world come about as you familiarize yourself with the inner world model of that person. And such resolutions often occur as if by magic. You do not have to discuss your work in the inner world with your adversary. In fact, unless you are very intimate with the person with whom you are having a conflict, it is a good idea not to reveal any of this work to them.

When working with people who populate your inner world, don't treat them as authorities. They may be a source of higher knowledge, but always bear in mind that they are, after all, only "human," with blind spots, flaws, and eccentricities just like the rest of us.

HEALING DIFFERENCES

One thing that becomes very clear in the study of the Lens of Perception is that each person has particular boundaries that are unique for him or her. The world created within each person's Lens has an integrity all its own, and recognizing this integrity in all people leads to self-validation and to the validation of other people. It is clear, in working with these principles, that the resolution of conflicts comes about not by working to dissolve the boundaries but by fully recognizing the importance of those boundaries and letting the other person know that you acknowledge and respect them.

When conflicts arise, caused by the coming together of two people with sharply different perceptions, the most direct resolution is achieved through *unconditional love*. Unconditional love is not *blind love*, that is, love that fails to recognize differences. On the contrary, unconditional love *consciously recognizes* the differences. To do otherwise would be to disregard the person's Logos-being, their purpose within the wide context of the Logos.

We are injured by clashes resulting from personal differences not because they are differences *per se* but because we feel that the person we are—our thoughts, feelings, dreams, aspirations, opinions—is not being seen or recognized. When this occurs, we feel "wiped out," or in danger of being wiped out. We feel that we are being threatened. After all, if the person with whom I disagree doesn't value the things that are important to me, or doesn't respect my right to value them, I might wisely assume that I cannot expect their support or encouragement. In fact, in any relationship with that person I should be alert about defending my own boundaries. This alert posture would be wise not so much because the other person would deliberately attack me, but because they can't see those boundaries. The principle here is that anything we don't respect or agree with tends to become invisible; it simply doesn't connect strongly with anything in our Lens of Perception. That is as true for you as it is for your adversaries.

Blind love that forgives all but does not acknowledge the differences can be at least as destructive and personally painful as conflict with a person who does acknowledge the differences.

Unconditional love—as distinguished from blind love—begins by recognizing the Lens of Perception that gives all people their personal boundaries. We have this in common with all people, and it is in this realization that we love. We need not always love the differences. In some cases we may even need to defend ourselves against them. But we can love that which we have in common—the fact that the Lens of Perception and all it entails is a necessary part of being human.

An Affirmation For Healing Conflict

I give myself permission to fully acknowledge and embrace my differences, knowing that these differences ultimately lead me to the fulfillment of my purpose in the Logos.

I give myself permission to fully acknowledge my adversary's differences. I know that I best serve the Logos when he/she also accepts and embraces the differences that lead him/her to fulfill his/her purpose in the Logos. I will do nothing to diminish that for either of us.

I give myself permission to trust the Logos, recognizing that it is not within my capacity to understand its plan for me or the plan for the person with whom I presently disagree.

Help me to find the strength to accept and protect my own differences while valuing this other person's differences, in the faith that the Logos has a larger plan for both of us which neither of us can see.

EXERCISE #4:

Getting What You Want From Life: The Art Of Manifesting

Purpose:

The purpose of this exercise is to increase your ability to bring positive change into your life. You will learn to do this by creating and managing images within your Lens of Perception.

Within the context of this exercise, the images you hold in your Lens have a two-fold purpose: (1) they act like a "homing device," keeping your attention focused on the things you desire so that you tend to be *drawn to* situations, people, or things that will assist you in making your dreams come true; (2) they act like a "psychological magnet," keeping your attention focused, so that you tend to *attract to you* situations, people, or things that will assist you in making your dreams come true.

MANIFESTING—NOT TOTAL CONTROL

Before proceeding with this exercise, I feel it is important to reflect on the nature of manifesting. This subject is often treated in a very glib fashion, with writers and workshop directors claiming that all you need to do is create a mental image of what you desire and that thing will come true. Although this initially inspires the reader or workshop participant, it often becomes discouraging, and the process quickly forgotten, when people attempt to apply it in their daily lives and it doesn't immediately work. I have found that rather than being given a simplistic inspirational technique, people do better when they see a larger picture of the manifesting process, with all its inherent weaknesses and strengths. Only then do they have the information needed to use the process successfully.

It is accurate to say that mental images do guide us in every activity in life. The principle here is that action follows intent, with intent being expressed in the form of a mental image, a daydream, or simply a desire to have something in your life that is not there right now. Put another way, the experiences we have in real life are reflections of the inner world of the Lens.

This is not to say that we deliberately or consciously recreate every element of the inner world in the external world. In order for this to be true, we would have to be able to exert total control over the world around us. For my mental images to come true for me they would have to override yours—which would be a kind of psychic tyranny, negating self-determination for everyone around us. It would be more accurate to say that the external world is a blending of the influences of our own Lens with the Lens of each and every person around us. In the larger scheme of things, the outcome is not wholly predictable. As Henri Bergson has said, we all participate in a much larger "order" than any one of us, from our own limited human perspective, can understand. We serve each other wholly only when our interests are mutual, only when the exchange between us is equal.

Your manifesting images actually act like a filter, sorting out that which serves you and dispensing with that which doesn't. By creating clear images of what you want, you draw to you those situations, objects, and people whose own needs *are served by the fulfillment of your dream.* Those who are not served are either repelled or are simply blind to your efforts.

There are many things in life that are great mysteries to us, which nevertheless profoundly affect our lives and limit self-determination. For example, we do not fully understand what purpose it serves for each of us to have a separate Lens through which we experience our lives, nor do we fully understand what purpose death serves in the scheme of things. However, both of these are facts of the human condition which we cannot erase simply by changing our inner world view. Similarly, it is difficult to be at peace with the daily news of war, famine, and the suffering of innocents. So far as we can tell, these are not things we "dream" for our world.

Regardless of who we are, our movements through life depend in large measure on the ability to grow and change. Part of this occurs automatically, part of it is self-determined. We grow and change through a three-step process: (1) recognizing where we are now; (2) clarifying where we want to go; (3) taking action to make dreams into realities in the external world. All three steps are made possible only through the Lens.

The following is a good example of the process.

Many years ago, a woman friend of mine, who I'll call Justine, decided that more than anything else in the world she wanted to become a doctor. From the time she realized this she could think of nothing else. She lived and breathed her dream.

At the time, she was employed as a nurse, and her family depended on her income. Furthermore, she had never done well in her science courses in nursing school, and she was afraid that she would be unable to complete the chemistry courses in medical school. To make matters worse, her husband was not comfortable with Justine's dream. He was content with the way things were and for a variety of reasons was opposed to his wife's pursuit of her dream.

In spite of the apparent obstacles in the path of realizing her dream, Justine literally could not put the dream aside. In her Lens, she was already a doctor, making her rounds at a hospital, helping those in need, and enjoying a respected role among her peers (this was very important to her). She decided that she would begin her journey toward the realization of her dream by fully embracing, fully believing in it. Almost daily, she created new pictures of herself in her Lens of Perception, working as a doctor in a great hospital. And each day, the mental movie of Justine as a doctor became more complete. Within a few weeks, she was thoroughly convinced that the dream was not only possible to manifest, she felt almost as though she had no choice in the matter. She *had* to become a doctor. It was in her blood.

She began taking night classes to make up for any deficiencies she might have in chemistry. And, motivated by the picture she had in her Lens, she passed these courses with flying colors. She continued to take courses at night school and on weekends, completing as much of her education as she possibly could outside medical school.

By the end of the first year, the changes that were occurring in Justine became noticeable to everyone around her. At her job she had greater self-confidence. She easily took responsibility for making decisions that were previously very difficult for her. Her new air of confidence and knowing had a positive effect on both her patients and co-workers.

Unfortunately, Justine's changes did not have an immediately positive effect in her marriage. Her husband was unable to share her dream, and in the end she made a decision to leave the marriage in order to dedicate herself to her medical education. Years later, I might add, both people agreed that the breakup had ultimately resulted in changes for which they were both quite grateful.

During moments of doubt, and especially during the months of her breakup from her husband, Justine felt that only her dream sustained her. She kept focused on that dream, and kept adding to the mental movie she was making of "Justine the Doctor."

Along the way there were many obstacles to over-come, and many of them appeared impossible at the time. When finally accepted into medical school, Justine was faced with the financial burden of doing this on her own. Thanks to scholarships and assistance from a relative—one whom she did not even imagine was in a position to help!—she was able to quit her job and devote her full attention to her studies. To make a long story short, Justine finally did become a doctor, and is presently practicing at a hospital in the midwest.

Justine's example, and the examples of many people like her, seems to prove that it is neither the presence or absence of obstacles nor the obvious presence or absence of resources such as money that determines a person's success. Rather, it is the power of the dream which a person holds in the Lens.

According to a theory developed by Dr. Albert Bandura and his students at Stanford University, there are certain *self perceptions* that lead people to success in achieving their goals, regardless of whether those goals are to stop smoking or to build a personal em-pire. The key of that perception is "self-efficacy," that is, the person's perception of their ability to do a specific task. Self-efficacy is determined by two things: (1) the ability to picture oneself as having already accom-plished his or her goal—and enjoying it!; and, (2) the ability to break down complex tasks, which taken in a single leap would be impossible, into smaller tasks whose accomplishment takes the person one step closer to the goal, while affirming his ability to accomplish what he sets out to do. For example, Justine would probably not have succeeded if she had decided that her first step was to divorce her husband, quit her job and enroll in medical school. However, she was able to perceive that she could immediately enroll at night school for the science classes she needed. Thereafter, she broke down the large task (completing medical school) into smaller tasks that she could perceive herself as easily accomplishing.

Self-efficacy feeds on itself. The outer reality of having accomplished a certain task supports and builds an inner reality of you as a person who can accomplish things. Your total organism—body, mind, and spirit—responds to your success with an improved capacity for self-efficacy. This process is important whether your goal is to lose ten pounds or to become president.

Always remember, manifestation is a reciprocal process, with your inner reality supporting changes in your outer reality, even while changes in your outer reality support your belief in the dream you hold in your Lens. In order for manifestation to work well for you, you must know how to both shape the dream on the Lens of Perception, and make changes in the external world that will support your dream.

Preliminaries:

Master the Triangulation exercise in this section of the book, or do some other deep relaxation technique that will allow you to focus your attention on the inner world.

➣ Schedule regular time, at least 15 minutes each day, to spend with the manifestation process.

➣ You will want a notebook to keep records of your work in the following exercise.

Instructions:

1. MAKE A "MENTAL MOVIE"

In a calm and even playful way, create a picture in your Lens of exactly what it is you want. Put yourself in the center of the picture, in the starring role. See yourself as you would be having already accomplished your goal. Make up imaginary conversations with any other people who might be involved. Always remember, you are in complete control of this picture. You may have people doing and saying whatever you wish them to say. Go through a list of your senses: sight, tactile sensations, taste, smell, and hearing, and attempt to use each one in your descriptions of the pictures you are making. For example, let's say you are making a movie of a vacation trip to Hawaii that you would like to take. Make a movie of yourself getting off the plane in Honolulu. Imagine the warm breezes against your face. Smell the aroma of the flowers. See and hear the surf as you lie on a warm, sunbathed beach. You will probably find that it is easy for you to focus your attention on some senses, difficult to focus on others. This is perfectly natural. Put your attention only on those that are easiest for you.

In creating your mental movie, don't be put off by the fact that you don't presently have all the resources you think you need for making your dream a reality. Don't let the fact that you cannot presently afford the trip to Hawaii prevent you from creating the mental movie. Surprisingly, the movie will make resources available to you in the future that you cannot even imagine becoming available to you right now. That is what manifesting is all about. It *creates* possibilities which you cannot even imagine right now. Then, when the movie is fully manifest in the real world, it will all seem logical, commonplace, and easy. Everything will seem to have been created from opportunities and resources which were there all along. The movie only brought those opportunities within reach, allowing you to make full use of them in your own life.

You do not have to create your mental movie in one sitting. In fact, it is better if you don't. Build on it a little at a time. Use time that would otherwise be "wasted"—waiting in line at the supermarket, on the bus going to work, and so forth—embellishing, adding scenes to this mental movie, always remembering that you are in total control of this inner world picture you are creating.

2. TAKE IMMEDIATE ACTION

Having gotten the production of your mental movie under way, look for a way to take immediate action. It is important that this be something you can do right now, with your present resources. For example, a woman who wants to make her workplace more beautiful might bring a flower to work and place it on her desk. A man who wants to go to Europe in the summer might go to a travel agency and start collecting brochures. Choose actions that you can do easily within the next day or two—and definitely choose actions that do not require you to complete a separate action before you can get to them. For example, don't make your immediate action going down to buy an airline ticket for your vacation if you must first save up the money for the ticket. Instead, make the immediate action getting the travel brochures. Only do what is immediately possible.

3. FOLLOW THE PATH OF LEAST RESISTANCE

The mental movie will focus your attention on objects, situations, and people who are important for the fulfillment of your dream. Be alert to all opportunities in the external world that make themselves available to you. Some of these opportunities will be obvious: the young man wanting to get a college degree, even though he must work full time, sees an ad in the paper for evening classes which he can attend; the woman starting a consulting business meets a person at a friend's home who could use her services. The fact that we have created the mental movie, and are constantly at work building it, makes these opportunities obvious to us. As this occurs, it is important to take action whenever the mental movie starts exposing opportunities to you: the person finding the ad for evening classes takes action by calling for more information and signing up for a class; the woman meeting a potential client at a friend's home takes action by telling the person she would like to phone her the next day to describe the services she offers. Trust the mental movie to guide you, and when it guides you to opportunities for fulfilling that movie in the external world, be aware that the opportunities are no accident. Take action.

4. PROJECT YOUR MOVIE TO THE EXTERNAL WORLD

Opportunities are not always obvious. When you first create your mental movies, it may not seem that anything is happening. Make certain that you are *projecting the movie into the external world*. For example, a young couple has worked together to create a mental movie of their dream house. Although they see many houses that meet their requirements, there appears to be no forward motion in terms of actually getting their house. The problem is that they have not yet told other people what it is they want. The external world does not realize what they want. So, they begin telling people what they want. They begin visiting real estate offices, going to open houses on weekends, talking to people about financing, telling friends and relatives. All these interactions with the

145

external world are ways of *projecting the movie into reality*, and as you do this the world becomes acquainted with what you want.

Projections need not be overly ambitious. At any given moment, do only what is comfortable for you to do—or which is only a tiny bit uncomfortable, a tiny stretch for you.

Let the mental movie be the engine pulling you along toward your dream, just as the locomotive of a train pulls it along toward the passengers' destinations. Your mental movie will do this, if you give it a chance.

SOME IMPORTANT TIPS

Being human, we are all prone to self-doubts, fears, guilts, and feelings of unworthiness that are expressed as a sense of incredulity about manifesting processes. Your success with the process will depend, in part, on your ability to counteract these emotional impulses. Remind yourself that everything created by human beings was created by the same process. Not everyone involved in the creation of, let's say, the chair in which you are now sitting, was aware of the process when he or she was doing whatever he did to make the chair a reality. The process was going on in that person's mind, however, whether he was drawing the original design or assembling the various parts that are necessary to complete the whole. Every action, be it getting up to walk across the room or creating a successful business, begins and ends with the process we have just described.

Self-doubts, feelings of unworthiness, guilt, and so on, will probably arise time and again. But understand that you have a choice about what to do with them. You may let them bring a halt to the production of your mental movie, or you may choose to ignore them. To ignore them successfully, simply remind yourself that you have complete control of the creation of your mental movie. The doubt or fear you feel will not stop you from creating that movie unless you allow it to.

When doubt or impatience arise, we often get discouraged and think to ourselves, "Maybe I better change the movie. This one isn't working." Note that if you do change it you are creating what I call a "moving target." Remember that your mental movie works two ways: it focuses your attention on possibilities in the external world, and it draws people to you who might help in the manifestation of that movie. If you keep switching the movie, you literally create a moving target. People who might assist you find the target too difficult to see—if they can see it at all. The one thing clear about moving targets is that they are always difficult to hit.

Sometimes you will choose to change your movie. But do keep in mind that by doing so you are creating a moving target and even good changes may slow things down for awhile.

THE LENS OF PERCEPTION

SELF-FULFILLING PROPHECIES AND MANIFESTING

There is a saying that "you must be very careful about what you dream because the chances are great that the things you dream will come true." This can be said about both our positive dreams (dreams of prospering, having good relationships, and so on) and our negative ones (fears of being poor forever or of never being able to find Mr. or Ms. Right, for example). Along these same lines, research with "self-fulfilling prophecies" has also shown that both the positive and the negative images we hold of people close to us tend to become manifest in that person. For example, the wife of the man who believes she is beautiful tends to become beautiful. And the child of the parents who believe him to be a poor student in school tends to become a poor student in school. To those ends, if we wish to be truly supportive of the people who are seeking to make positive changes in their lives, we must look at the present image we have of them and seek to create a new image in our Lens that will be in full agreement with that person's goals. Thus, the husband who wants to support his wife in her goal of becoming more beautiful must do so by creating an image in his Lens of his wife as already being more beautiful—in his eyes. And the parents who wish to support their son's desire to be a better student must do so by creating an image in their Lens of the son already being a better student.

The inner world does impose itself on the external world, bringing about change—either positive or negative.

ANNOTATED BIBLIOGRAPHY

The following books have been particularly meaningful to me in writing this book:

Alice's Adventures In Wonderland
By Lewis Carroll, published by Bantam Books.

Written originally for children, this literary classic was my introduction to the reality of the inner world. Carroll understood the lens of perception as a kind of theater or mental movie, whose ability to entertain was limitless. Prefacing *Alice's Adventures* is the line "In fancy they pursue/ The dream-child moving through a land/ Of wonders wild and new,/ In friendly chat with bird and beast—/ And half believe it true."

Reading Carroll's work is the most enjoyable way I know to become acquainted with life in the inner world.

The Teachings of Don Juan
By Carlos Castaneda, published by Ballantine Books.

I have always believed that Castaneda's work, like Lewis Carroll's, was best understood as tales of the journey inward. The "Yaqui way," described in this book, is to embrace the inner world as the true "reality," with the external world being the "illusion" with which we can hope to make only fleeting and imprecise contact.

Castaneda's books have entertained and stirred the imaginations of millions of readers. But more important, I think, is the fact that the author's adventures with Don Juan have taught us all the spiritual value of the inner world.

The Brain Revolution
By Marilyn Ferguson, published by Bantam Books.

By the author of *Aquarian Conspiracy*, this book is a highly readable, but well researched exploration of human consciousness and human perception. It helps link modern brain research with spiritual transformation, teaching much about "perceiving ourselves in the act of perception."

Beyond Biofeedback
By Elmer & Alyce Green, published by Delta Books.

This is a basic book for the study of human perception as it affects human physiology. Written in an easy to understand, and at times entertaining style, it presents the pioneering biofeedback research directed by Elmer & Alyce Green at the Menninger Clinic. Although originally published in 1977, the material presented here still holds up, and provides a very convincing, scientifically documented picture of the effects of our perceptions on our ability to find pleasure in life, to perform difficult physical feats easily, and to heal ourselves when we are ill.

The Way Of The Shaman
By Michael Harner, published by Bantam Books.

A general introduction to shamanism, a system of thought where the exploration of the inner world is perceived as a central pathway opening into *reality* & where self-understanding ultimately leads to the revelation that whether we choose to acknowledge it or not we have a powerful spiritual link with the Universe.

You Are Not The Target
By Laura Huxley, published by Tarcher.

This book inspired me to develop and teach techniques for more fully using the resources of our inner world. In this book Laura describes what she calls "recipes for living and loving," creative visualizations, and other techniques, that show us how to make better use of the inner world, for solving both large and small issues in our lives. This might well be considered Part II of the "workbook" for *Lens of Perception*.

Memories, Dreams, Reflections
By C. G. Jung, published by Vintage Books.

I have learned more from Jung than any other single writer about human perception and exploring the inner world. For him, the human consciousness was "a vast uncharted territory," more exciting than the external world. For Jung, the inner world was shaped by numerous influences—environmental, spiritual, and cosmic. This inner world literally becomes our lens of perception, and through this lens we look at an external world we can never hope to "know." The interaction between the inner and outer determines the quality of our lives, and becoming familiar with that inner world is the key to self-fulfillment.

Working With The Dream Body
By Arnold Mindell, published by Routledge & Kegan Paul.

The author of this book is a therapist and teacher at the Jung Institute in Zurich. He is one of the leading proponents of dream and body work, bringing about personal transformation through the process of exploring how dreams, and our perceptions of reality, affect our bodies. This book explains the general principles for working with these concepts in a therapeutic setting or for self-growth.

Soul Return
By Aminah Raheem, Ph.D., self-published, Aptos CA.

Part of human perception, according to Raheem, is passed from generation to generation through the "soul". This book has been meaningful to me in exploring how and why there is a continuity and evolution in human thought, human emotion and human perception. This book has taken me far outside psychological perspectives on the human experience, with startling glimpses into the reality of the eternal.

Seven Arrows
By Hyemeyohsts Storm, published by Harper & Row.

This book has done more than most to introduce shamanic thought to the modern world. The message in this book that was most important to me was the idea that we each have a unique lens of perception. Although this lens may distort reality, it is only by embracing and discovering the pictures we produce on that lens that we can fully enjoy, and allow the rest of the world to enjoy, the gift we can make manifest through that lens. Storm shows how the gift of the inner world is expressed in dreams, visions, animal and ancestoral guides, and through story telling.

Sophocles: The Oedipus Cycle
Edited by Dudley Fitts & Robert Fitzgerald, published by Harvest Books.

The ancient Greeks had a vision of human perception and its limits that not only made excellent drama but gave us much to ponder on the nature of perception itself. Reading Oedipus, I saw for the first time how our own perceptions are the raw materials for what the Greeks called our "fate."

ABOUT THE AUTHOR

Hal Zina Bennett, Ph.D. is a consultant, author and teacher. He works with individuals and organizations to assist them in discovering, embracing and expressing their inherent inner guidance and creativity. He offers short and long-term consulting.

He is the co-founder, with Susan J. Sparrow, of PATH: Inner Resources, established for the purpose of researching the intuitive arts and developing tools for accessing inner resources.

As a leading author in holistic health and human potential, he has published more than a dozen books, including the ground breaking *Well Body Book*, with Mike Samuels, M.D.

Write the author for information about consulting services, lectures or personal appearances.

Hal Zina Bennett, Ph.D.
P.O. Box 60655
Palo Alto, CA 94306

Definition:

(33)
(131)

"Logos"-being

131 Blind spots, flaws, eccentricities

reality is inevitably altered by the presence of the observer.
(advanced physics)

pg. Cheyenne Shaman
94 Hyemeyohsts

then "quantum leap" in our